YOUR VIRTUAL CLASSROOM

LEARNING ZOOM, GOOGLE CLASSROOM, AND OTHER ONLINE TO___
ONLINE CLASS

SCOTT LA COUNTE

RIDICULOUSLY
SIMPLE BOOKS

ANAHEIM, CALIFORNIA

WWW.RIDICULOUSLYSIMPLEBOOKS.COM

Table of Contents

Disclaimer: *Please note, while every effort has been made to ensure accuracy, this book is not endorsed by Zoom Video Communications, Inc., Google LLC, Slack Technologies, Inc., InVisionApp, Inc, or Atlassian Corporation Plc and should be considered unofficial.*

INTRODUCTION

Teaching has never been easy. Taking your teaching online can complicate this. This book is *not* about how to make the switch and strategies to use in your classroom, rather it is about the tools you will more than likely use.

Every school is different. Some will use Google Meet, some will use Zoom, and some will use some other tool, so I've tried to include as much software as possible. The focus, however, will be on Google-related software.

The book covers

- Zoom
- Google Meet
- Trello
- Slack
- Chromebook
- Google Apps
- Google Classroom

ZOOM

[1]

WELCOME TO ZOOM

This chapter will cover:
- Zoom's pricing model
- What makes Zoom unique
- How to sign up

UNDERSTANDING ZOOM PRICING

The first question most people are going to have when they sign up for Zoom is probably a financial one: should I pay? Zoom's free plan is a full-feature product. In fact, almost all of this book will cover features that you don't have to pay for!

So, why on Earth would you pay for something that's free?

The answer to that largely depends on how you will be using it, so this section will cover which plan is right for you.

The biggest caveat of the free plan centers around the meeting duration limit: it's 40-minutes (unless you have less than three people).

The free plan is limited to one host and 100 users. That's probably plenty for most people. If you need more, then that's where an upgrade will help. Enterprise plans can have up to 1,000 participants on a call.

The next level up from free is the Basic plan ($14.99 per month per host). This lets you host meetings for up to 24-hours—but seriously, if you're hosting a 24-hour meeting, then maybe it's time you take a vacation because that's intense! You also get a personal meeting ID which comes in handy if you have the same meeting every week. This way you can give people a link for where the meeting is happening instead of having to give everyone a link more last minute each time it happens. Finally, you can record a meeting to the cloud (on the free plan, you can record a meeting locally—i.e. on your computer's hard drive).

For most small businesses, the Basic plan will work out great. There are two big features that might make upgrading to the Pro plan ($19.99 per month per host) beneficial: one, the pro plan bumps you up to 300 participants; and two, you can have your own company branding—that may be useful if you have a lot of clients and you want your meeting to have a more high-end feel.

It should also be noted that Zoom also offers plans specific to different industries like Education and Telehealth.

Finally, it should be noted that there are premium Zoom add-ons. The biggest one is for webinars. You could technically host one through your free or paid account, but there is a $40 per month webinar plan that offers features like Q&A and the ability to show the webinar live to Facebook or YouTube.

ZOOM VS. GOOGLE MEET (FORMERLY HANGOUTS)

The next question a lot of users will probably have is why Zoom? There are other videoconferencing companies out there. Zoom is perhaps the best known, but what about Google Meet? That's free and integrates perfectly into your Google Account.

It really comes down to you and your business. Google Meet is amazing software. It's great for smaller meetups—and can even handle larger ones.

The biggest difference between the two comes down to features. Google Meet is very basic. It's stripped of almost all the features that will be covered in this book. That might work out well for short daily scrum calls, but hosting a larger meeting that needs breakaway meetings will be more problematic.

There are also smaller details—like Google Meet doesn't let you have a custom background, which has become the favorite feature of many Zoom users.

SIGNING UP

Signing up to Zoom is pretty straightforward.
Go to Zoom.us and click the signup button.

The first thing you'll see is an age verification form. I know some people like to lie about their age, I don't recommend it here—especially since this is all private—but if you do it, make sure you do it in a way that you are over 18.

For verification, please confirm your date of birth.

| Month ˅ | Day ˅ | Year ˅ | Continue |

This data will not be stored

If you add an age younger than 18, then you'll be greeted with a message about not being eligible to sign up for Zoom.

That message won't go away if you refresh your browser; the only way to clear it so you can sign up is to clear your cache or use another browser.

Once you add your age, you'll need to either add your work email (i.e. the email clients and colleagues contact you) or sign in with SSO (for users that are logging in to a company's custom Zoom domain—most users will not use this), Google, or Facebook.

I recommend Google. There are no passwords to remember. But it's really up to you. Using one or the other doesn't give you any account benefits within Zoom.

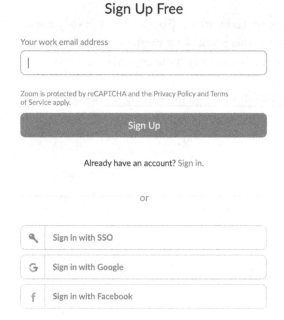

If you choose Sign in with Google, then it will ask you what Google account you want to use.

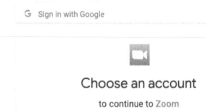

Once you're signed up, you'll see your account dashboard.

Free and paid accounts will have a similar look and feel. I'll be using a free account for the first part of this book, and then switching to a paid account to cover some of the admin features (like user and room management).

If you decide to upgrade at any time, there's an option on the top that says Plans & Pricing that outlines all the various plans.

[2]
Getting Started

This chapter will cover:
- Editing your profile
- Setting up a meeting
- Meeting options
- Meeting templates
- Settings

Editing Your Profile

Once you sign up for Zoom, you are technically ready to go—you can start your first meeting right away.

I recommend holding off on that and updating your profile first. You can do that by clicking on Profile to your left.

Anything that can be changed has a blue Edit option next to it (or change for profile picture). The reason I recommend going here is twofold: one, if you used your personal email account, it may have an avatar that you don't want work people to see, or it may have a nickname instead of your real name (for example, mine says "Scott Douglas," which is my pen name for many books); two, you may need to update the time zone—this will make sure you don't miss meetings (if you get a scheduled meeting and you have the wrong time zone listed, then you'll get the wrong time and will miss the meeting).

When you click the Edit next to your name, you'll also be given the option to add things like your phone number, job title, and your location. It's all optional but may be beneficial depending on how you are using the account.

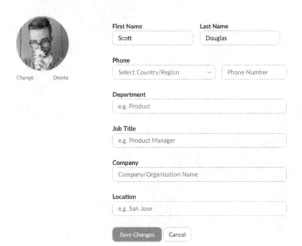

Near the bottom of the profile page is a place to sync your calendar; that way if you get invited to a meeting, then you'll see it in your Google Calendar (or whatever meeting you have synced).

If you change anything here, make sure you save it.

HOSTING YOUR FIRST MEETING

Before you can start a meeting, you have to schedule a meeting. Don't worry: if you want to start it right away, there's going to be a way to do it. But you still have to start with scheduling it.

To get started, go to Meetings on your right, and click the blue Schedule a New Meeting.

Next, add in your meeting details. Technically, you don't have to do anything here. You can just accept all the defaults. But adding details will help make the meeting more identifiable. For example, having a unique name like "Morning Standup Call" is going to help when you have several meetings scheduled. If you are on the free plan, you'll also see the warning about 40-minute calls.

Near the bottom, there are two things of particular note. One is the option that says Video. This does not mean that this will not be a video call. It just means the video is turned off when people first join. This is recommended so people have time to adjust themself before people see their face. The second thing you should pay attention to is the Meeting Options. If you want people to be able to join in before you get there, for example, you can check off the first option to Enable join before host. You can also mute everyone as they arrive. Finally, you can Record the meeting automatically on your computer (if you don't check this off, then there's an option to record once the meeting has begun). Once you have everything saved, select Save.

After you save your meeting, you'll see it as an upcoming meeting. From here you have the option to delete it or to start it. So if you want to start it ASAP, then just click Start.

MEETING OPTIONS

Before looking at what happens when you start a meeting, let's look briefly at the three other meeting tabs in the Meeting menu.

If you see something in this book that isn't in your version of Zoom, the reason is very likely the setting is toggled off. Toggle it on, and restart the software, then you should see it.

PREVIOUS MEETING

As the name implies, the first option shows all of your previous meetings. You can delete any of these, or you can start them again.

PERSONAL MEETING ROOM

I said that you need to schedule a meeting before starting a meeting. This is technically true, but there is an option to start what's called a personal meeting. This is more of a private one-on-one meeting. It's sort of what you would do more on the fly—an unscheduled meeting to go over something briefly.

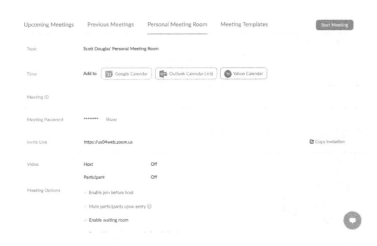

MEETING TEMPLATES

Meeting templates help you save time by saving common meetings. Let's say you have a lot of ten-minute scrum meetings. You can save one meeting as a template and then just copy that template anytime you want to start a similar meeting.

By default, the tab is obviously blank because you haven't saved any.

If you go into your upcoming meetings or previous meeting then click the name of any meeting, you can open up the meeting details. Scroll to the very bottom and you'll see an option to save the meeting as a template.

Save as a Meeting Template

If you return to Meeting Templates, then you'll now see an option to schedule the meeting with the template. You can save up to 40 templates.

SETTINGS

The last section under the Personal menu is for settings.

When you access this area, you'll see a tab menu across the top with three options: Meeting, Recording, and Telephone.

Meeting   Recording   Telephone

I'm going to go a little backwards in this second because most of the things we are covering are in the first area. Very briefly, however, let's look at the other two menus: Recording and Telephone.

Recording is where you can go to change by whom and how an online conference can be recorded. You can also toggle on and off if you want it to record automatically and if you want a disclaimer so anyone joining in knows they are being recorded.

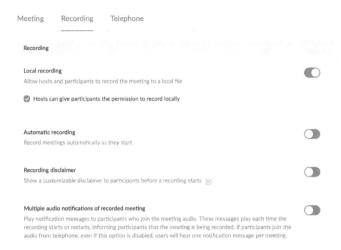

The last menu, Telephone, contains just two options that are both just on / off toggles. One is to show international numbers on the invitation email and the other is to hide phone numbers of people calling in.

SETTINGS (BASIC)

Most of the meeting settings are just toggles and they're self-explanatory. There are a few worth pointing out in a little more detail, however. The first are under the Basic Settings menu.

The Chat feature is something you should pay particular attention to. Depending on the users, you might want to have it off entirely. I'll go more into how chatting works on Zoom later in this book, but for now, just know there are options here to limit it.

Anything with a V next to it means it's only on certain versions of Zoom—usually 4.0 or later: at this writing, version 5.1.0.

In Meeting (Basic)

Require encryption for 3rd party endpoints (SIP/H.323)

By default, Zoom requires encryption for all data transferred between
the Zoom cloud, Zoom client, and Zoom Room. Turn on this setting to
require encryption for 3rd party endpoints (SIP/H.323) as well.

Chat

Allow meeting participants to send a message visible to all participants

☐ Prevent participants from saving chat ☑

Private chat

Allow meeting participants to send a private 1:1 message to another
participant.

Auto saving chats

Automatically save all in-meeting chats so that hosts do not need to
manually save the text of the chat after the meeting starts.

Sound notification when someone joins or leaves

Under File Transfers, there is an option to limit what can be sent; if, for example, you only want
Word files shared—not photos or videos—you can save it there. To allow only certain files, check off
the Only allow specific file types.

Show Zoom windows during share screen is more of a preference; by default when you are sharing
your screen doing a presentation, you can't see anyone else; toggling this on shows you participants.

File transfer

Hosts and participants can send files through the in-meeting chat.
☑

◯ Only allow specified file types ☑

Feedback to Zoom

Add a Feedback tab to the Windows Settings or Mac Preferences dialog, and also enable users to provide feedback to Zoom at the end of the meeting

Display end-of-meeting experience feedback survey

Display a thumbs up/down survey at the end of each meeting. If participants respond with thumbs down, they can provide additional information about what went wrong. ☑

Always show meeting control toolbar

Always show meeting controls during a meeting ☑

Show Zoom windows during screen share ☑

Screen sharing

Allow host and participants to share their screen or content during meetings

I'll cover annotations and whiteboards later, but be aware that by default people can save these; if you don't want them to, uncheck the box.

Who can share?

◉ Host Only   ○ All Participants ⑦

Who can start sharing when someone else is sharing?

○ Host Only   All Participants ⑦

Disable desktop/screen share for users

Disable desktop or screen share in a meeting and only allow sharing of
selected applications. ⒱

Annotation

Allow host and participants to use annotation tools to add information
to shared screens ⒱

☑ Allow saving of shared screens with annotations ⒱

☐ By default, only the user who is sharing can annotate ⒱

Whiteboard

Allow host and participants to share whiteboard during a meeting ⒱

☑ Allow saving of whiteboard content ⒱

☐ Auto save whiteboard content when sharing is stopped

If you are doing any kind of survey in your conference, then Nonverbal feedback is an option you might want toggled on; it lets users nonverbally give feedback by clicking on buttons.

Remote control

During screen sharing, the person who is sharing can allow others to
control the shared content

Nonverbal feedback

Participants in a meeting can provide nonverbal feedback and express
opinions by clicking on icons in the Participants panel. ⒱

Allow removed participants to rejoin

Allows previously removed meeting participants and webinar panelists
to rejoin ⒱

Allow participants to rename themselves

Allow meeting participants and webinar panelists to rename
themselves. ⒱

Hide participant profile pictures in a meeting

All participant profile pictures will be hidden and only the names of
participants will be displayed on the video screen. Participants will not
be able to update their profile pictures in the meeting. ⒱

SETTINGS (ADVANCED)

I'll cover Breakout Rooms later in this book; these special rooms give you the ability to have mini sessions within your conference. For example, 100 people join your meeting; 30 minutes into it, you can have a breakout session of 10 groups of 10; they go off and have mini sessions, then return to the main room after. To use them, make sure you toggle this on (it's off by default).

Closed captioning is also an option here. If you want people to read what the person is saying, then toggle it on here; keep in mind, however, someone has to manually type the captions.

Report participants to Zoom

Hosts can report meeting participants for inappropriate behavior to Zoom's Trust and Safety team for review. This setting can be found on the Security icon on the meeting controls toolbar. [v]

Breakout room

Allow host to split meeting participants into separate, smaller rooms

Remote support

Allow meeting host to provide 1:1 remote support to another participant

Closed captioning

Allow host to type closed captions or assign a participant/third party device to add closed captions

Save Captions

Allow participants to save fully closed captions or transcripts

Far end camera control

Allow another user to take control of your camera during a meeting. Both users (the one requesting control and the one giving control) must have this option turned on.

Most people love virtual backgrounds—or at least don't get upset when other people have them. Some people find them unprofessional and annoying. If you are of the latter, you can disable anyone from using them here.

Virtual background

Customize your background to keep your environment private from others in a meeting. This can be used with or without a green screen.

☑ Allow use of videos for virtual backgrounds ⓥ

Identify guest participants in the meeting/webinar

Participants who belong to your account can see that a guest (someone who does not belong to your account) is participating in the meeting/webinar. The Participants list indicates which attendees are guests. The guests themselves do not see that they are listed as guests. ⓥ

Auto-answer group in chat

Enable users to see and add contacts to 'auto-answer group' in the contact list on chat. Any call from members of this group will be automatically answered.

Only show default email when sending email invites

Allow users to invite participants by email only by using the default email program selected on their computer

Use HTML format email for Outlook plugin

Use HTML formatting instead of plain text for meeting invitations scheduled with the Outlook plugin

I mentioned earlier that you need to install Zoom software to use it; that's not entirely true. The host can actually enable users to use their browser by toggling this on. It's off by default because many features are not available in the web browser based version of Zoom.

Allow users to select stereo audio in their client settings

Allow users to select stereo audio during a meeting

Allow users to select original sound in their client settings

Allow users to select original sound during a meeting

Show a "Join from your browser" link

Allow participants to bypass the Zoom application download process, and join a meeting directly from their browser. This is a workaround for participants who are unable to download, install, or run applications. Note that the meeting experience from the browser is limited

SETTINGS (OTHER)

If you want other people to schedule meetings on your behalf, you can assign a person by adding their information in the Assign scheduling privilege to section.

Blur snapshot on iOS task switcher

Enable this option to hide potentially sensitive information from the snapshot of the Zoom main window. This snapshot display as the preview screen in the iOS tasks switcher when multiple apps are open.

Invitation Email

Your meeting attendees will receive emails in language based upon their browser/profile settings. Choose languages which your expected attendees will receive content in to edit.

Choose email in language to edit   English   ⌄   ✏

Send me a preview email

Schedule Privilege

You can assign users in your account to schedule meetings on your behalf. You can also schedule meetings on behalf of someone that has assigned you scheduling privilege. You and the assigned scheduler must be on a Paid plan within the same account.

Assign scheduling privilege to   +

No one

[3]

YOUR FIRST VIDEOCALL

This chapter will cover:
- Starting a meeting
- Basic meeting features
- Virtual background
- Chatting in Zoom
- Breakout sessions
- Changing window views

STARTING A MEETING

To start any meeting, find the meeting and click the Start Meeting button. But what about the people that are attending it? You have two options:

One, open the meeting by clicking on the name, and then scrolling down until you see the invite link.

From here, click the Copy Invitation option. This brings up a box with the meeting information. Click the copy button again, and then go into your email and create an email to the people who are going and paste this message inside of it.

The second option requires you to download a small add-on for either Outlook or Chrome. This lets you schedule meetings right in your Outlook or Google Calendar.

The next thing you'll see is the Zoom software with a message asking you to join with Computer Audio. You can click the option below that if you want to test your audio first.

ZOOM CONFERENCE BASICS

Now that the person has their invite, let's start a meeting and see how to use it.

The first thing you will see is a box asking you to open Zoom. Zoom requires software on your computer—it is not cloud-based. Assuming you have it, then click the open button; if you don't, then click the Download option on the webpage.

The next thing you'll see is the Zoom software with a message asking you to join with Computer Audio. You can click the option below that if you want to test your audio first.

At this point, you have the option to invite people to the conference. Or you can wait for them to show up.

Invite Others

When someone comes, you'll see a message with their name and the option to remove or admit them. You can also click Message to send them a note—such as the meeting will start in five more minutes; until you click Admit, they are in a virtual waiting room and cannot see what's going on in the conference.

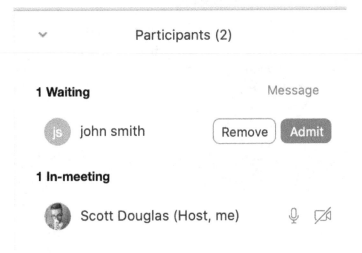

MICROPHONE SETTINGS

Most people will not want to change the microphone settings; it should update automatically based on your computer settings.

If it fails to do so, however, you can manually set both the microphone and speaker settings. To do so, click the up arrow next to the microphone icon when you are inside a conference room.

This will bring up a menu that shows all the available devices that you can connect to.

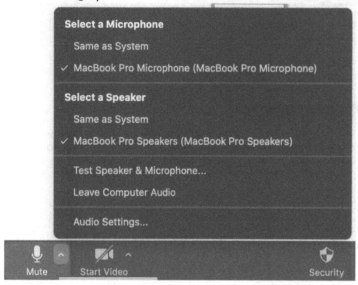

At the bottom of your screen are the main Zoom options. The first two are Mute and Start Video. If there's a red line on the icon, that means the feature is turned off. In the example below, my video is turned off but my microphone is not—so people can hear me, but not see me. You can toggle them on and off by clicking them one time.

Next is Security. This lets you select what options you are giving people who join the conference. If, for example, you want people to come into the room without you admitting them, you can click Enable Waiting Room. Keep in mind, however, that if your link was public, people can log into the conference that you don't want. We'll go over these features in more detail later in the book, so don't worry about fully understanding them now.

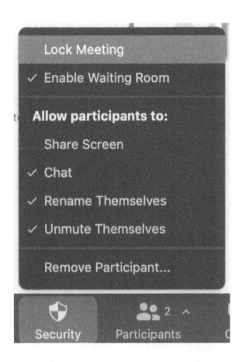

Participants opens a list of everyone in the room; Chat lets you talk to people in the room; Share Screen lets you show people what's on your computer screen—this is used if you are presenting something; and finally, Record lets you record the meeting.

To end the meeting, click the End button.

MUTING ALL

One of the most helpful features in Zoom is the Mute and Mute All. Sometimes people forget to turn their microphones off during a meeting—or there's a dog bark that's disrupting the meeting. Whatever the case, you can click on the Participants icon, then hover over the person and click the microphone next to their name; alternatively, you can go to the bottom of this screen and Mute All, to mute everyone.

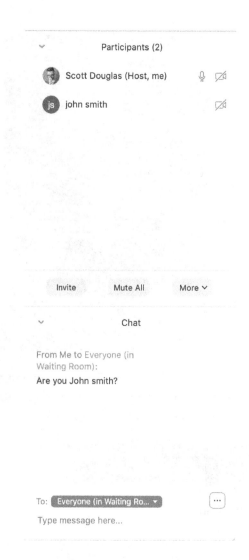

VIRTUAL BACKGROUND

The edge Zoom has over most videoconference companies is the amount they invest in more personable features. This is especially true with the popular Virtual Background feature. This lets you alter your screen to make it appear like you are somewhere besides your office.

To change your background, click the arrow next to video, then select Choose Virtual Background.

If you've never done this, you'll have to download a quick package the first time.

Once it's done, click the Plus button next to Choose Virtual Background. This will let you find a picture to use (hint: if you don't have one, go to google.com/image and search for Zoom backgrounds). The one I am using here is the couch from The Simpsons.

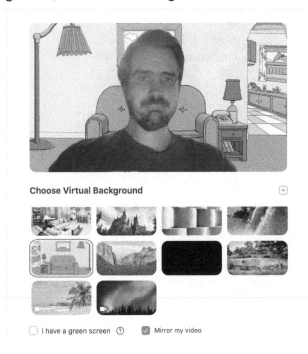

Once you have selected it, close the box. If your video is toggled on, then you'll see it immediately; if it's off, then toggle it on. This background will remain when you start the next meeting, so be careful! You may have a fun background for a more casual meeting that you want to turn off when you have a business meeting.

RENAME USER

Sometimes you don't want to show your full name; or maybe you're sharing Zoom with a spouse and their name is coming up instead of yours. Renaming is pretty easy in Zoom.

Click Participants on the bottom menu bar, then go to your name and click "More"; finally select Rename.

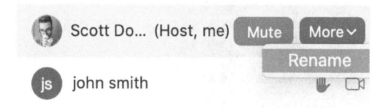

Add whatever name you want, then select the Rename button.

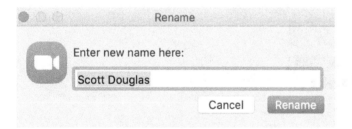

CHATTING IN ZOOM

To start a chat, click on chat in the Zoom bottom menu. By default, when you chat on Zoom, everyone in the room sees it.

Chat

If you click on Everyone, you can select one person you want to chat with. This changes the group chat to a private chat, which means only you and the other person can see it—not everyone in the conference.

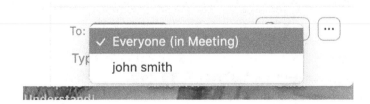

You can confirm it is a private chat by the red text that says (Privately).

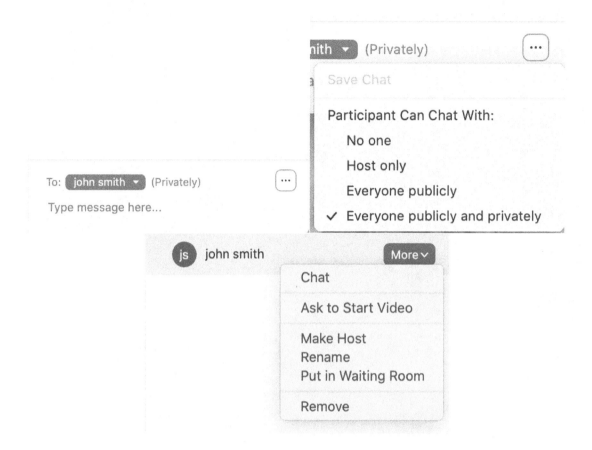

BREAKOUT SESSIONS

Breakout sessions are mini-conferences within larger conferences; as mentioned earlier, you have to turn the setting on for this to work. So if you don't see the room option, refer to the settings section and confirm that you have toggled it on.

Once you have enabled it, there are two ways to use the feature: during the conference and before the conference has started. I'll cover both ways below.

Create a Session While the Conference Is Going

When you enable Breakout Rooms, you'll see a new Breakout Rooms icon when you start your conference.

When you click the icon, you'll see options for how the room is going to be created. It can either be created automatically or manually; if it's automatic, then people are randomly assigned to the number of rooms you create. For example, if you create two rooms and ten people are in your meeting, then each room will have five people.

Once the rooms are created, you'll see a list of all of them. You can add a room by clicking the button at the bottom, or click Recreate to reset everything.

If you click on Options, you'll get several choices. By default, a person has to manually accept that you are putting them in a room; the first option puts them in the room automatically. You can also put a timer on the length of the breakout sessions—by default, you must manually close the rooms. And finally, the last option lets you decide how long people have to leave the rooms after you close them. It's a good idea to leave it at at least 60 seconds to give people time to finish thoughts.

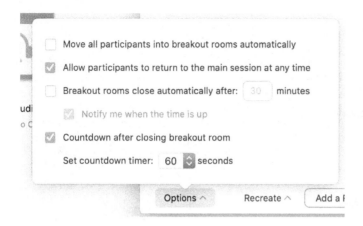

To assign someone to a room, click Assign, and then select the person's name that you are assigning.

Once they are assigned, you can see all the people in each room. When you are ready to start a breakout session, click the blue Open All Rooms in the lower right corner. If you close this box, all your settings can be saved. So you can create your Breakout Rooms early in the conference, and have them ready to go for later.

Once the Breakout Rooms begin, you can check the progress of who has (and has not) joined.

As the host, you are not in a Breakout Room. You have the ability to pop into any Breakout Room that you have created to check out how things are going.

If you want to leave the Breakout Room, click End, and then select the blue Leave Breakout Room; this will return you to the main conference room.

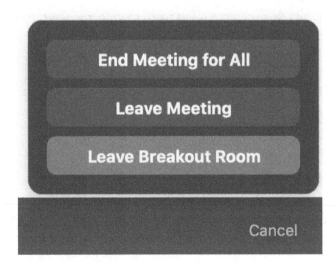

You can also broadcast a message to everyone that is inside of a Breakout Room. Click the Breakout Room icon, then select Broadcast a message to all from the lower left corner.

If you have not put a timer on the Breakout Rooms, then you will have to close them manually. To do this, click on the Breakout Room icon, then click the red Close All Rooms button.

You'll see a message on your interface that tells you how long users have to return to the main room. Some users will probably end early, so you will slowly start seeing them reappear in your main room.

ASSIGN BREAKOUT ROOMS BEFORE THE CONFERENCE

You can also create Breakout Rooms in advance. This can be great for small businesses where everyone is using their work email. It can be problematic, however, when everyone is using non-work email; you may have one email, then the person joins the conference with another email—so when the breakout sessions start, they don't get assigned.

If you'd like to pre-assign the rooms, then schedule a meeting as you normally would. Under Meeting Options select Breakout Room pre-assign.

Meeting Options   ☐ Enable join before host

                         ☐ Mute participants upon entry 🔒

                         ☑ Enable waiting room

                         ☐ Breakout Room pre-assign

                         ☐ Record the meeting automatically on the local computer

When you select the option, you'll have two options: Create the rooms manually or import them from a list.

☑ Breakout Room pre-assign

     + Create Rooms   ⬆ Import from CSV

When you create it manually, you'll get an empty box with no one assigned.

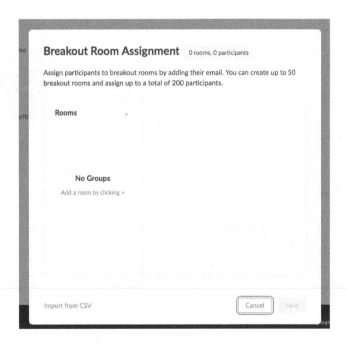

To add a room, click the + icon next to the rooms.

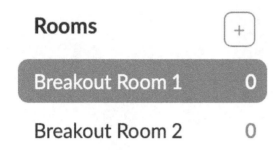

Once a room is added, you can click the pencil icon to rename it.

To add someone to the room, just add their email under Add participants and hit enter.

Once you save your changes, you'll see how many rooms are assigned in your meeting notes; you can select Edit to change it.

When you manually add people, you will need to upload a CSV file (you can export in CSV format from Excel or Numbers) using Zoom's template. When you click the import option, there is an option to download their template.

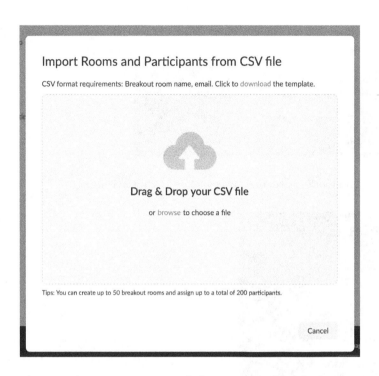

The template is pretty straightforward; one field to name your room and one field to say who is in that room. You can add and remove rows from the template.

breakout_room_template

Pre-assign Room Name	Email Address
room1	test1@xxx.com
room1	test2@xxx.com
room2	test3@xxx.com
room2	test4@xxx.com
room3	test5@xxx.com
room3	test6@xxx.com

WINDOW VIEWS

There are several different window views for Zoom—but people have to have their video turned on to use them. So, if you're in a meeting and don't know why some of these views don't work, see if everyone is using video for the conference.

To get started go to the upper right where it says Gallery View. That's how you toggle between all the views. The open box next to Gallery View will turn your software into full-screen mode.

In full screen, you can move the thumbnail video preview boxes around your screen.

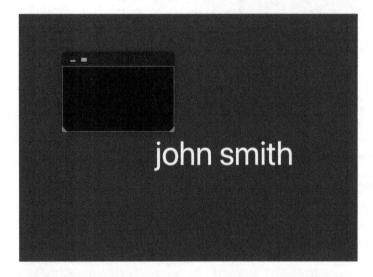

You can also minimize the boxes by clicking on the minus.

There are two views: Gallery View where you see everyone, and Speaker where you see the main speaker in a large box.

When your software is in full-screen mode on a Mac (in Gallery View), you can go to other software and have your conference windows appear as a picture-in-picture view.

[4]

ADVANCE CONFERENCE SETTINGS

This chapter will cover:
- Conferencing settings
- Sharing your screen
- Whiteboards
- Managing people in a room

ZOOM CONFERENCE SETTINGS

There are two types of settings in Zoom. There are settings in your account; and there are settings within your conference. We covered the first settings earlier. This section will cover the second part of settings, which you can get to when your conference is open; click the drop down and select Preferences.

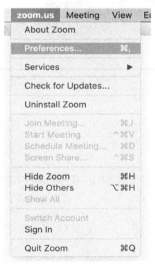

You'll see almost a dozen different settings that you can control. Don't worry! These are all very basic settings. And most are pretty self-explanatory.

Under General, you can select multiple monitors (if you have your laptop connected to another screen, for example); you can also change the skin tone of your reactions.

Under Video you can change the ratio and change how Gallery View is organized. You can also have it touch up your appearance...just remember, it's not a miracle worker! What this feature does is create sort of a light blur on your face to hide blemishes.

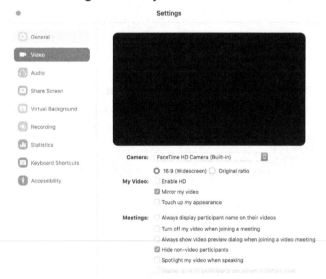

At the bottom of the Video options menu, you can get a few more options when you click the button.

If you are having trouble with your mic, you can go to the audio settings and see if it's working. When you speak, you should see the input level lighting up; if you aren't seeing that, then there's probably a problem with your mic.

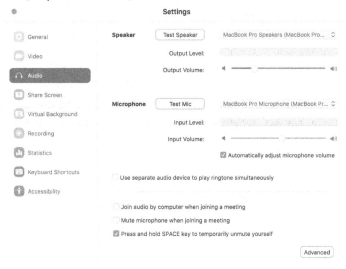

Share Screen settings updates how it looks for both you and other participants when you share your screen.

There are a few more options when you click on the Advanced button.

If you are recording a meeting, you can select where it's being saved in the Recording menu. You can also separate the audio of each person who speaks, which is good if you plan on editing the file later.

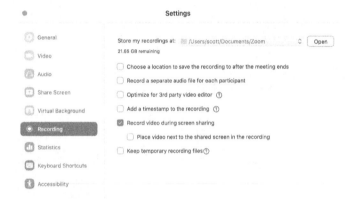

Statistics isn't very helpful unless you are having a connectivity problem; you can use this setting to see how you are connected—if you have bad bandwidth for example. It's good for troubleshooting if there's a connection problem on your end or another person's.

Keyboard Shortcuts lets you change the default shortcut for any function with a different key.

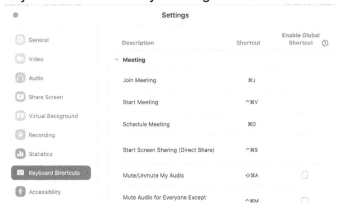

To update a shortcut, click the shortcut section and add what key command you want to use.

Accessibility is for adjusting how subtitles look—you will need to update your subtitle preference from the main setting menu as well.

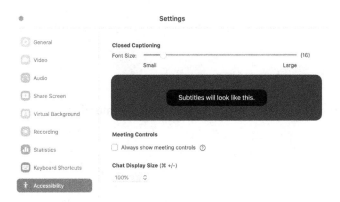

SHARING YOUR SCREEN

As the host, you can share your screen; you can also control if other people can share their screen as well.

Click the Share screen button in your bottom menu, and you can get started. The first thing it will ask is what you want to share. You can share your desktop (meaning whatever is on your computer screen), a specific window on your desktop, a Whiteboard (covered in the next section), or a device window such as an iPhone.

If you click the tab above, you can go to Advanced settings. From here you can select only a portion of your screen you want to share, if you only want to share sounds coming from your computer, or if you want to use a second camera.

Finally, the last tab lets you share files from your computer to everyone in the meeting.

On the bottom of any of these screens, you'll see two options: one to share your computer sound (if you are sharing a screen with a video, for example, you'd want to make sure this is on); two, to optimize your screen.

☐ Share computer sound   ☐ Optimize Screen Share for Video Clip

ANNOTATIONS AND WHITEBOARDS

Under the share screen, there's also an option for a Whiteboard. A Whiteboard is a place where you can draw notes for everyone to see. It's a great way for brainstorming because others can draw on the board as well.

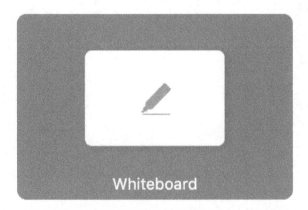

The functionality of the Whiteboard is very basic; you can write text on it, draw or stamp. You can also use the Spotlight button to call attention to something.

Drawing gives you several prebuilt things you can add—such as circles and squares.

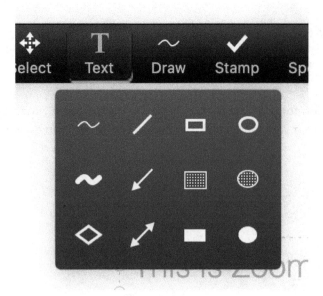

Remember, everyone sees the Whiteboard and everyone can add to it; so it can get a little messy quickly.

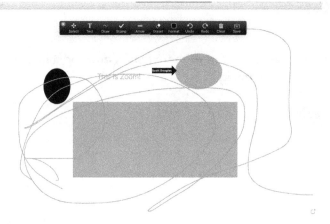

MANAGING PEOPLE IN A MEETING

As the meeting host you have the ability to manage what people can do. For example, if a person has their video turned off, you can go to More, and select Ask to Start Video.

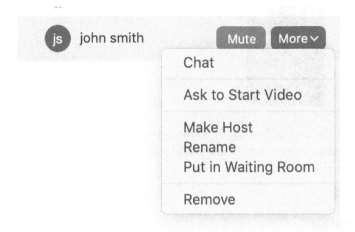

You can also mute them.

Or if they are muted, you can ask them to unmute themselves.

On the other end, the users in your meeting will be able to click a raise hand button; this is a way for them to ask a question without disrupting the meeting. You'll see a hand-raise next to their name and can acknowledge them whenever you want.

REACTIONS

When everyone has their videos turned on, they can also give reactions to the person speaking. You'll see it in your bottom toolbar tray as the last option. If you don't see it, confirm the video feed is on.

You can give two reactions: clapping and thumbs up.

Other users will see it on their screen like the image below. Reactions can be used to keep people on mute while getting acknowledgment that they approve or understand something. When everyone has to unmute to give opinions, it can disrupt the flow of the meeting.

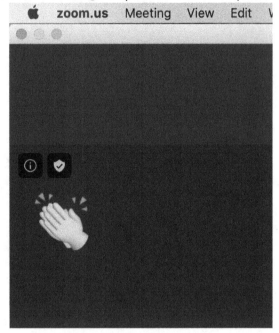

Paid Features Only

Chances are you started Zoom on the free plan. Why not? The free plan is full of the most powerful features offered in the paid plan. So why switch? The biggest reason is probably meeting duration—nobody wants to be 39 minutes into an hour meeting only to be told your plan doesn't allow for longer than 40 minutes. All the paid plans have unlimited meeting durations.

There are other benefits to the paid plan; notably, you get a custom meeting ID, cloud recording (so no more taking up hard drive space storing meetings locally), and daily reports on how employees are using (or not using) it.

If you get to a place where you want to pay for Zoom, there are two things you want to pay attention to on the bill screen. One, if you pay yearly (all months up front) then you get a discount. And two, you need to pay for each host. What does that mean? It means if you have one host, you can only have one meeting happening at a time. If you need multiple meetings, then select the number of hosts you need.

You'll also see a number of paid add-ons—if, for example, you plan on doing webinars.

[5]

MANAGING ZOOM

This chapter will cover:
- User management
- Group management
- Room management
- Account management
- Webinars

USER MANAGEMENT

Once you pay for a subscription, several areas on the left side that have been closed will now be open. The first option is User Management.

Under User Management you can add people to your account. Just click the +Add Users button (blue) or do an import if you have a long list of users. You can also come here to search for users.

When you add a user, you can give them either a Basic or Licensed plan and also add a description of who they are.

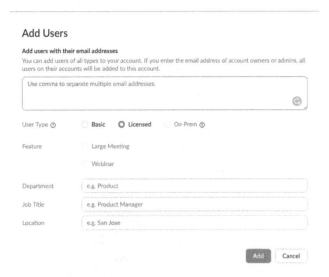

Once you add them, they'll get an email from you asking to confirm they want to be added. You'll see their name in Pending until they accept the invitation.

Finally, under Advanced, you can change the User Type for all members.

GROUP MANAGEMENT

Group Management helps you organize all your members; so, for example, you can have your IT people in one group, and Admin people in another. Then when you schedule a meeting, you can add that entire group instead of finding each person one by one. Click the blue +Add Group to get started.

This will ask you to name the group and give it a description.

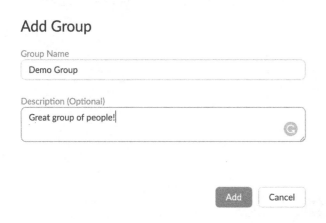

Once you click Add, you will see your group, and can click the +Add Members button in the lower right corner to start putting people in the group.

Just type their email, then click Add.

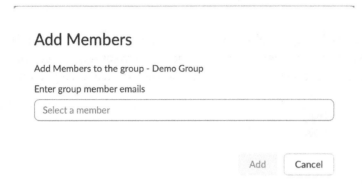

ROLE MANAGEMENT

Under Role Management, you can give admin roles to different people in your organization. Click the blue +Add Role button to get started.

Next, add their role, then click Add.

ROOM MANAGEMENT

When you have a paid account, you are also able to create private rooms with unique lock codes; to add one, go to Zoom Rooms, and select the blue +Add Room button.

Next, add your unique security code.

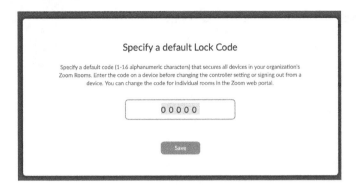

CALENDAR INTEGRATION AND DIGITAL SIGNAGE

Within Room Management there are two final options: Calendar Integration and Digital Signage Content.

Calendar Integration is pretty easy to understand—just plug in Google Calendar or whatever calendar system you use.

Digital Signage Content might be new to you. When you think of Zoom, you typically think about having a video conference; Zoom Rooms go beyond that. Digital Signage lets you use your computer like a billboard. Think about going to a fast food restaurant—those digital menus are really just digital signs.

You could technically hook up a large computer to it, but you can also buy very thin HDMI sticks for less than $200. A quick search for "Mini PC Stick" found the one below for $149. It's literally a computer that's only a few inches—small enough to fit in your pocket! You could stick one of these into your HDTV and no one would be able to see it.

STORAGE EXPANSION OPTIONS

To add digital signage just click on the option to manage your displays.

When you add a room under Zoom Room, there's a drop-down option for digital signage display.

Add a Zoom Room

Room Name

This field is required.

+ Add a Calendar

You can add a calendar service for easy arrangement for your Zoom Rooms' meetings.

Room Type

Digital Signage Only

Zoom Room

Scheduling Display Only

Digital Signage Only

Once you have the room added, add your location. Once the room is added, you'll get an email with the activation code. Open the computer you are going to show the signage on, open up Zoom, and add the code. It's pretty simple—much more simple and cheaper than many of the digital signage companies out there!

Once your location is added, you can go to digital signage and start adding your content. There are companies that will create content for a fee, but many people just create it in PowerPoint or Keynote using a template, then export it as a JPEG.

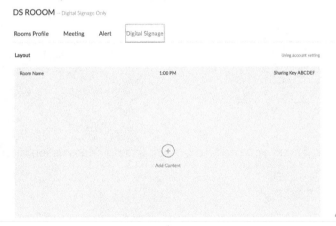

When you add content, you can create a playlist of sorts; so you can schedule exactly when the content will play. You could have it showing a lunch menu until 3:00, then switch automatically to a dinner menu at a set time.

ACCOUNT MANAGEMENT

Account Management is important for one important reason: It's where you can cancel, edit, or upgrade your plan. Once you have an active plan, you can click the Cancel or Edit button at any time to remove or update the subscription.

Below this screen is also were you can add various add-ons (such as webinars).

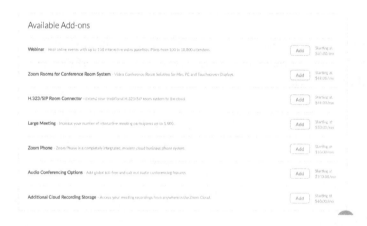

Under Account Management you can also get reports on Zoom usage by user.

And add instant messaging groups.

ADVANCED

Advanced has a lot of features most people will not use. You can add Branding, for example (but at a premium price) and extra security (again, at a premium).

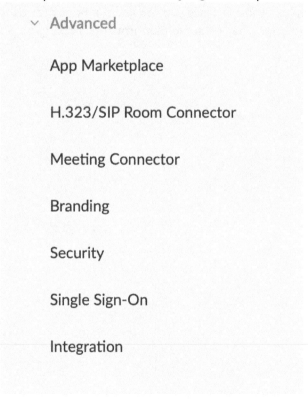

What you will find under Advanced that you might use is Apps. Just like your phone has apps, so does Zoom; these are mini add-ons (many are free) that enhance Zoom. Adding the Slack add-on, for example, let's you open up conferences within your Slack channel.

WEBINARS

Webinars probably won't be for most users. At $50 a month, it's only something you want to add when you are read to actually host Webinars.

The advantage of hosting a Webinar here versus other places is you can charge money for people to attend it. There are also most extra features you don't see on some platforms—like taking polls and adding your own branding.

GOOGLE MEET

[1]

GOOGLE MEET OVERVIEW

This chapter will cover:
- What is Google Meet?
- How to join a meeting

INTRODUCTION

Google Meet (or Google Hangouts as it used to be known) is Google's answer to videoconferencing. The powerful tool integrates right into any Google Account—that means if you use Gmail or your employer uses Google Account, it's ready for you to use.

The simple yet robust tool is perfect for individual meetups and group conferences. Best of all: It's free!

JOINING A MEETING

To get started, you can either use the Google Meet link provided by the person who is calling you or go to meet.google.com and click the green Join or start a meeting button.

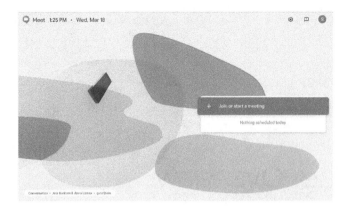

If you choose to join a meeting manually, then you will need to copy and paste the meeting name into the box, and then click Continue.

Depending on your computer, you will probably see a message about giving Google Meet permission to use your computer's camera and microphone. It is important to accept these permissions! If you fail to do so, you will need to log into the meeting again.

Once you start Google Meet, you will see what your computer's camera sees, and a note about any people that are already in the meeting. You are not in the video call at this point! This is a chance to preview the video feed that your colleagues will see and make any adjustments. When you are ready to enter the meeting, click the green Join now button.

[2]

GOOGLE MEET ENVIRONMENT

This chapter will cover:
- Navigating Google Meet
- Chatting
- Sharing screen

You should see a screen similar to the one below when you join your call. Your main screen (the largest video) will show whoever is talking. This means if you talk, everyone will see your video here. Remember to mute your mic (see instructions in this guide) to prevent your video from being mistakenly shown here. Google Meet cannot distinguish between a person asking a question, and a person who has loudly shifted in their chair, so remember to mute your mic unless you need to ask a question or verbally participate in the conversation.

The bar on the bottom of your screen is the area you will interact with the most.

Starting from left to right on the bar, the first button is the meeting name. When you click this button, you will see the meeting link for the call and other information.

The next three buttons are: microphone, hang up, and video. If either your microphone or video button is white, then they are turned on. If you click them one time, it is turned off and the button icon turns red. If you are experiencing poor internet connectivity, turning off the video may help. If you are not speaking, then it is advisable that you keep the microphone button off; this will help keep Google Meet from mistakenly thinking that you are talking, which can interrupt the flow of the meeting.

The Turn on captions will transcribe what the person is saying into text. This feature is not perfect, and it is important that you listen to what the person is saying and not just read the captions.

Turn on captions

There may be a point when a person asks you to present your screen (for example you are showing a presentation for a meeting). If that happens, then you will need to click the Present Now button, and then click Your entire screen.

This will take you into a present mode where your entire screen is shared. Make sure to close all other windows to keep other people from seeing something that might be private to you. When your presentation is over, click the Stop presenting button.

To the far lower right corner, there are three vertical dots; this is the settings / options menu.

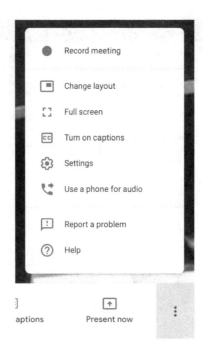

Starting at the top of this menu is the Record meeting option; when you click this, the class will be recorded for you. Before the recording begins, you will see a screen about asking for consent. Before recording a call, ask the other person on the call for permission. Once you finish recording a call, the recording will be emailed to you. It may take several minutes to appear in your inbox.

Ask for consent

Recording a meeting without the consent of all participants may be illegal and actionable. You should obtain consent to record this meeting from all participants, including external guests and guests who join late.

Decline   Accept

By default, the layout of the call is set to Auto. This means as more people join / leave the meeting, the layout will be resized for optimal viewing. If you prefer to adjust the layout manually, you can do so by clicking the Change layout button in the options menu.

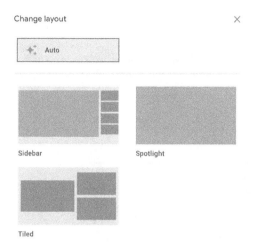

If you are using a wireless headset (such as AirPods or other Bluetooth headsets), then you can click Settings in the option menu to select an alternative microphone / speaker. Make sure the device is connected before going into Settings.

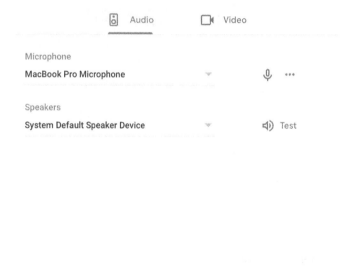

If for any reason you are not able to use the microphone on your computer, you can click the Use phone for audio button in settings to switch audio to your phone. You will still be able to see the meeting on your screen, but your phone will serve as your microphone.

The Report a Problem button in the options menu is not for reporting problems internally. If you use the feedback forum here, no one on the call will see it; the forum is sent to Google. This forum is only to report performance issues that you want Google to know about.

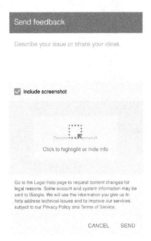

In the upper right corner, there are two buttons that you can click. If you click the button with the two people, you will be able to see a list of everyone on the call.

The button next to the people (an icon of a chat message) will launch the call chat feature. To send a message, go to the bottom of the window, type your message, then use the arrow button (or hit the enter key).

Send a message to everyone

People use this feature to paste web links and other information that's being discussed in the call; it's also used to ask questions, so you don't interrupt the person speaking. Everyone sees the chat! This is not private.

To leave Google Meet, it is your responsibility to click the hang up button in the middle bottom portion of your screen; alternatively, you can wait for the other person to end Google Meet, which will force everyone out automatically. Once you leave Google Meet the light that is illuminated next to your computer's camera will turn off; that means it is no longer recording video. If you still see the camera light, restart your computer to force it to turn off.

You left the meeting

Rejoin   Return to home screen

How was the audio and video?

☆   ☆   ☆   ☆   ☆

Very bad   Very good

SLACK

INTRODUCTION

It didn't seem so long ago that instant messaging and texting in the workplace was not only frowned upon but outright banned. Times have changed. Chatting online is now not only part of workplace culture, but the preferred way teams communicate.

When it comes to this type of communication, there is one service that rules them all: Slack.

Slack lets you communicate with your company, and teams within the company, in a way that is private, secure, and fun! This book will teach you what you need to know to use the popular service.

[1]

WELCOME TO SLACK

> This chapter will cover:
> - What makes Trello unique
> - How to sign up
> - Changing background

SETTING UP YOUR WORKSPACE

The first thing you need to do is set up your "workspace"; your workspace is the environment that your team will collaborate in. It's where they'll share files, messages, calendars, and more.

You can get native Slack software for your computer, phone, or tablet—or you can just run it from your web browser. Before you download anything, however, you need to get your account running. Head to slack.com to do that, then click the Get Started button in the upper right corner.

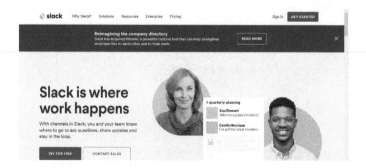

The next screen will ask you if you are setting up a workspace for your team or if your team is already using it. If your company already has a Slack channel, then you can sign in and jump into the conversation after accepting the team's invite. If you are creating the environment, then select the first option: + Create a Slack Workspace.

Next, add your work email. What's a work email? It's the email with your business domain, but if you are using a gmail or yahoo type email address.com, that's fine.

Once you add your email, Slack will send you a confirmation email; just paste the code in the boxes below and you are all set.

Next, name your company. This is going to be the name of your workspace as well, so keep it professional.

The next question is about what you are working on. This will be your first "channel" which we'll cover later in the book. You'll probably have several channels for different teams. Pick one and add it here. Common channels companies have include channels for software bugs, company news, and happy news; there's no wrong channel, so use this space for whatever you want and call it whatever fits your company.

Finally, you can start inviting people to your project. Alternatively, you can skip this step and add them later.

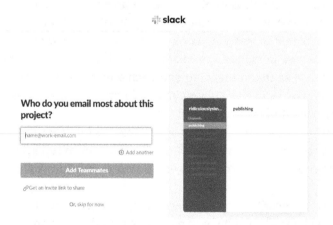

The next screen is a screen telling you that you're done.

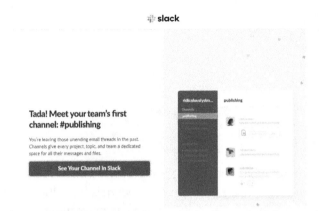

Once you click See Your Channel in Slack, you will see the workspace.

WHY PAY?

Like a lot of software, you probably will start using Slack and be quite happy with the free plan. It's doing everything efficiently. So why would you pay for something that works great? It really comes down to how you will use it.

As you start using Slack, there's probably going to be a point where you want to search for a message. Slack saves the past 10,000 messages on the free plan. That sounds like a lot, but this isn't email—this is more like instant messaging. Look at your phone—how many text messages did you send yesterday? The average person will send around 70. If your company has 30 people, that's 2,100 text per day. So if Slack is like text messaging and each employee is sending 70 messages per day, then you'll hit 10,000 messages in about a week! So you can only see a message from a week ago! On the paid plan, it saves unlimited messages.

Free plans also let you integrate ten tools; again, this is a lot, but the longer you use Slack the quicker you'll see how fast these tools will add up. You have unlimited integrations with the paid plan.

Paid plans also let you create shared channels so people outside your organization can communicate.

Finally, there's a lot of security and compliance features built into the paid Slack, so if you're in an industry that requires enhanced security, you may have no other option.

What you really have to ask yourself is how much those features are worth to you. Paid plans start at a little under $7 per user. So a company of 30 will be paying a little more than $200 a month. They have different options, so my advice is to talk to a Slack salesperson if you want to switch to paid to see if they can offer you a better plan.

[2]

CHANNELING SLACK

This chapter will cover:
- What makes Trello unique
- How to sign up
- Changing background

WHAT IS A CHANNEL?

Slack Channels are what make Slack unique and efficient. Within a company, there might be hundreds of channels with different themes, but each employee will only follow the ones most relevant to them.

For example, the marketing team will have their own channel, then there probably will be a general channel for all company news.

You'll see all your channels on the left side. Click on any of them to enter the channel and read messages.

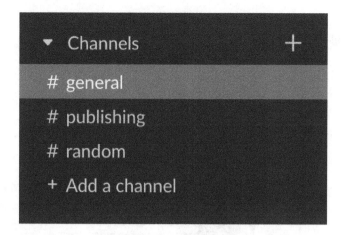

Channels can be public (meaning any employee can find them) or private (you need to be invited to join). Note: if you make a private room, you cannot make it public later.

Most companies usually have channels that are more personal (where employees share personal milestones or things that made them happy) or a place for things that made them laugh. Remote teams especially know the importance of having fun in Slack—sharing the lighter side of the news.

FIND CHANNEL

When you click the + sign next to channels, you'll get two options: browse channels and create channels. To find a channel, click the Browse channels option.

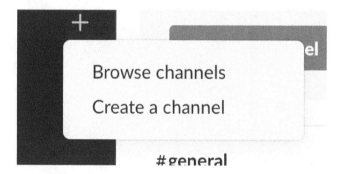

Once you are in Browse channels, you can search for the channel you want to see or see a list of all the channels.

You can also ask a person to send you a link to the channel. To create a link, right click on the channel name, then select Copy link.

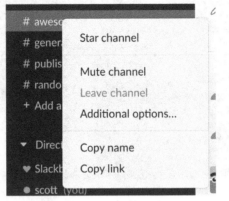

CREATE A CHANNEL

To create a channel, click the + sign again and select Create a channel. Next, add in the relevant information. Only the name of the channel is required, but a description is beneficial if people will be searching for it, or if the name doesn't clearly show what the channel is for.

LEAVE A CHANNEL

You cannot leave the main General Channel, but you can leave channels that were created internally by the company. Right-click on the channel you want to leave, then select Leave channel.

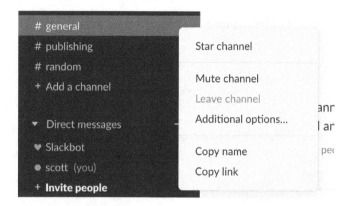

ARCHIVE / DELETE A CHANNEL

There are two things to do with a non-active channel: delete it or archive it. Delete removes it entirely—all the messages will be gone and people can no longer search for them (files will remain, however); if you archive it, people can still search through it, but no one can add anything to it or join it. Unlike deleting a channel, you can undo an archive—so if you change your mind later, then you can put it back.

To delete or archive a channel, right-click the channel, then select Additional options.

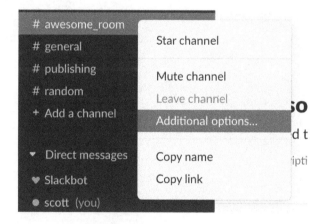

Next select what you want to do: Archive or Delete. You can also go here to change the channel name or make it a private room.

Additional Options for #awesome_room

Archive this channel

If you don't think it will be used anymore and you want to clean up, archive it. The channel can be unarchived later (but everyone will have been removed).

Change to a private channel

Private channels can only be joined if you are added by a current member — they won't show up in your channel browser. This change can't be undone.

Rename this channel

You can rename a channel at any time. But, use it sparingly: it might confuse or disorient your colleagues!

Set the channel description

Channel descriptions are especially useful to new members choosing which conversations to join.

Delete this channel

Deleting a channel will permanently remove all of its messages. This cannot be undone.

→

[3]

MESSAGES

This chapter will cover:
- What makes Trello unique
- How to sign up
- Changing background

WRITING MESSAGES

Writing a message is pretty easy. If you've ever written an email, then you know 90% of what you need to know.

To write your first message, click on the channel you want to write the message in (remember, a message is only seen in that channel—you don't write a message that's seen in all channels).

Near the bottom of the channel, you'll see a box to add your message. There's a toolbar with most the things you are already used to (e.g. bold text, italicize, strikethrough, add a link, etc.). Once you type your message, hit the send button on the right side to post it.

So what's different? First, notice the @ on the right-hand side? That brings up who can see this message (you can also manually type these—for example, "@here"); when you post a message, anyone can open the channel and see it, but if you add @here in front of your message, then anyone who is logged into Slack will get a notification. If you type @channel, then everyone who belongs to the channel will get a notification; and if you add @everyone, then everyone who belongs to the Slack workspace will be notified—even if they aren't in the channel.

To the far-left side is a lightning icon. Click that for a list of shortcuts you can create in your message. We'll cover these shortcuts later in the book.

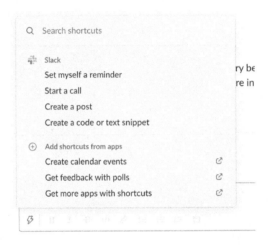

Editing Messages

Once a message is posted, you can go back and edit it if you made a mistake or want to change what you said. Click the three vertical dots to the right side of the message, then select Edit message.

Change what you want to, and then select Save Changes.

Reply to a Message

If there's a question on the channel, you could technically just reply by typing a new message in the channel. Some people do that. It creates unneeded noise in the channel, however. The best way to reply to the message is to hover over it, then go to the menu bar that appears, and click the second icon (the chat icon).

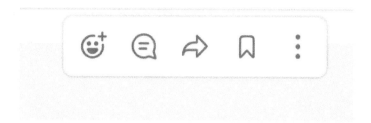

This turns the message into a thread; so people don't see the back and forth that might follow unless they are following the thread.

If it's a message that doesn't need an answer, but the person wants acknowledgement that you saw it, you can use the first icon—the emoji. You can add a thumbs up, or any number of other emoji reactions; this shows up when a person looks at the message but doesn't interrupt everyone to say that you replied.

SEARCHING FOR A MESSAGE

On top of Slack is a search bar. You can use this to search through all Slack messages or just in a specific channel.

Once you get your searches returned, you can narrow them down by dates, users, or channels.

DIRECT MESSAGE

Direct messages are private messages that you have with other employees. There's a caveat here, however—your boss has a right to read them. They are able to see even private messages. Does that mean they do? Some do; some don't. Some will but only if there's a lawsuit. The best advice here: don't have a private conversation in Slack that you would be embarrassed by.

To start a direct message, click the + sign to the right of the Direct Message menu; next, type the employee's name. When you see it appear, double-click it. That opens up the exchange between you and the other employee.

TALK TO YOURSELF

Lastly, Slack lets you talk to yourself! Under Direct Messages you see your name? That's where you can type to yourself. It's a good place to send yourself notes and attachments.

[4]

SLACK CALLS

This chapter will cover:
- What makes Trello unique
- How to sign up
- Changing background

If you do a lot of video calls, you can skip Zoom or Google Hangouts and go directly through Slack to make the call. Personally, I find it a little slower than dedicated video software, but it really depends on your needs.

To start a call, start a message with a person, then click on their name. This brings up a small box with their mini-profile. Select Call to get started.

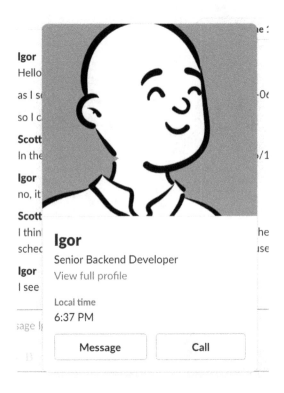

Depending on what system you are using, there's probably going to be one or two extra steps to enable your microphone and webcam. Just answer the questions you see on your screen.

SCREEN SHARES

Once you're on a call, you can also share what's on your screen by clicking on the middle button.

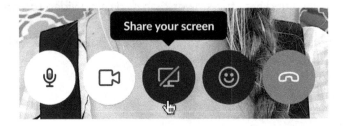

By default, your teammates are going to be able to draw on your screen to point things out while you're presenting; you can turn it off by clicking on the group drawing icon. You can also draw on your screen to call attention to things by using the Pencil icon.

[5]
ACCOUNT SETTINGS AND APPS

This chapter will cover:
- What makes Trello unique
- How to sign up
- Changing background

There aren't a lot of settings that you'll want to change in Slack, but I'll call out some of the more important ones.

CHANGE STATUS

When you are working on a remote team, it's important to keep everyone up-to-date on if you are actually working. It's not required. It's polite. If someone asks a question, it lets them know that you're away on a call or taking a coffee break.

In Slack, there's no need to tell everyone in the room what you are doing. Just change your status so when they see your name, they'll see a little note.

To change the status, go to the upper left side and click your name. Next, click Update your status.

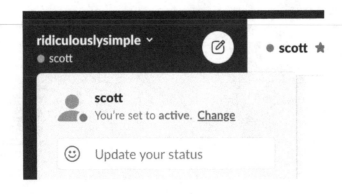

Slack is going to have a couple of status updates that you can pick from, but you can also write your own by typing it in the box—you can also click the smiley face emoji to update the graphic that shows next to your status.

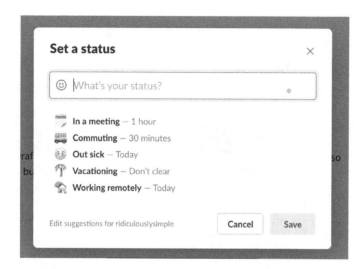

Once you save it, it will ask you when you want to clear the status (meaning it goes back to the normal status).

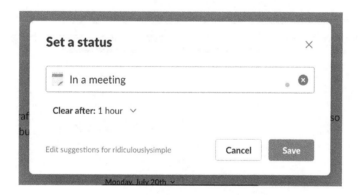

CHANGE PROFILE

To change the profile that people see when they click your name, go to the left side where the instant messages are, and click your name. Then click it one more time and it will bring up a small box. Click Edit Profile.

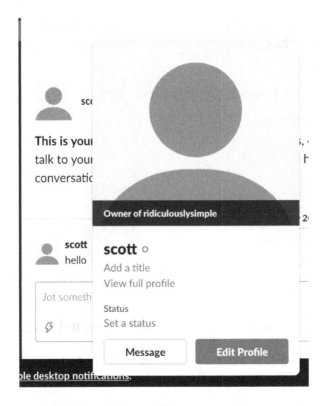

You can add whatever information you want. It's helpful to add a photo of yourself and describe what you do, but nothing is required. You can also update your time zone here.

ACCOUNT SETTINGS

In the same place you went to change your profile, you probably noticed a little sidebar open on the right side. That's where you can go to edit your account settings. This will look different if you aren't the workspace owner. Click the More button, then click Account Settings.

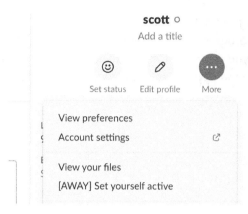

From here you can change things like your password and language. You can also click Access Logs over on the right to see who has logged into your account.

ALERTS AND REMINDERS

While in account settings, you can also click the Notification tab to change how you get alerts. If you want email notifications, for example—or if you just want a pop up on your computer.

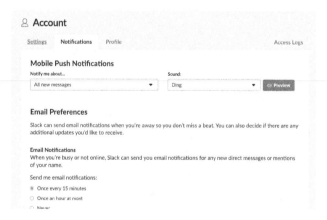

SLACK APPS

Slack is one of the most used communication apps in the world, so it probably isn't a surprise that there are literally thousands of Slack apps.

You can see them by going to slack.com/apps.

Apps are integrations for programs you already use. So if you use Google Apps (like Google Drive to share files) or Zapier, then you can plug it into Slack and work it within the Slack app.

To install an app just go to the apps page, find the app, then click install.

INTRODUCTION

Working as a team can be challenging, but working remotely as a team can add a layer of complexity to the work; it can be difficult to monitor who is working on (or responsible for) different aspects of a project and where they are in terms of deliverables. Trello, which is a part of the enterprise software development company Atlassian, is a Kanban-style project management tool that can run natively on your computer or on the web.

Trello lets you work collaboratively wherever you are and whatever you are working on. There are free and paid versions of the software, so it works for any budget and any company regardless of size. It also integrates with the software you already have.

TRELLO

[1]

WELCOME TO TRELLO

This chapter will cover:
- What makes Trello unique
- How to sign up
- Changing background

THE BASICS

To get started, head to https://trello.com and sign up for a free account.

The sign-up is a breeze. You can sign up with your email or just use your Google, Microsoft, or Apple account to login. Personally, I prefer to use one of those three to login because it will be one less password to remember.

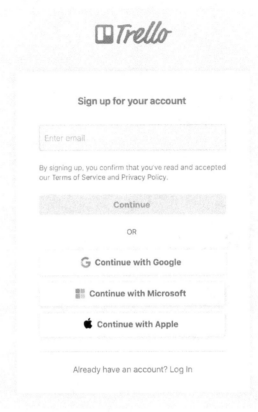

You'll get a confirmation about who you are (you'll also get an email—emails will come from Taco, which is probably one of the stranger email senders you'll have in your inbox). Depending on how you are signing in, you'll probably have an extra layer of verification you'll need to add (i.e. a verification code).

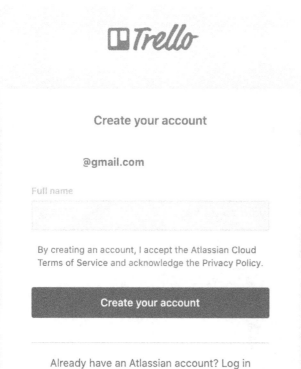

That's it! You'll now get a very brief onboarding tutorial. Here you can create your first board (Don't worry! You can delete it).

You'll probably have several boards. You may have one for your sales team, one for your admin team, etc. Within those boards, you'll have different lists. Within that list, you'll have different cards.

Add the name of your board. I'm just going to call it my vacation planning board.

Click the grey button; it will turn blue when you do this. When ready, hit the blue button to go to the next step.

Next, you can start naming your lists. You'll be able to start with three, but you can add more later. You'll notice as you do this, there will be a preview that changes.

Next, you can start naming those cards within your to-do list.

As you do so, you'll again get a preview of the changes on the right side.

Finally, you can add details within the list—this will be things like descriptions, checkboxes and attachments.

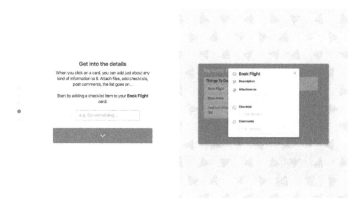

The last step just tells you that you are ready to go.

Once you click keep building your board, you'll see the full Trello board.

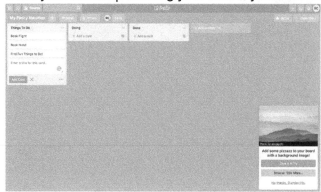

Before continuing, I'll pause to point out that this book covers the web version of Trello, but Trello has a native Mac and Windows app, and native mobile app. They all work exactly the same. And they all sync together! So if you do something on your iPad, it changes on the web version. Why use a native version (vs. the web version)? It's a little more intuitive and responsive.

Trello works seamlessly wherever you are.

Web

Mobile

Desktop

CHANGING YOUR BACKGROUND

I'm sure you are just dying to get into the wonderful world of boards, but before we do so, let's give Trello some personality by seeing how to change your board background.

One note before I show you this: everyone sees your background who is a member of your board. So if you are sharing a board with a team, you probably don't want to change the background to your personal family photos. For private boards, have fun! For business boards, it's usually best to stick with neutral colors.

To get started, open up the board you want the background on, click the Show menu... button in the upper right. Finally, select Change Background.

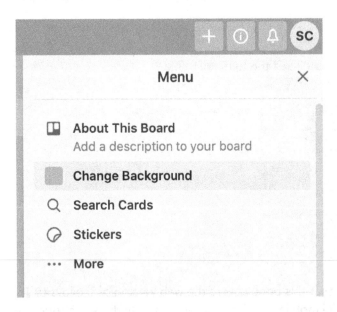

You have three choices: Photos, Colors, and Custom. Custom is only for paid subscribers and it lets you add your own photos (not the stock photos I'm about to show you).

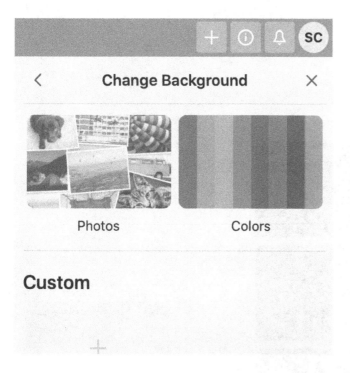

When you click Photos, you'll see dozens. You can search for what you are looking for or just browse. When you find the one you want, click it, then click the X in the upper right corner.

Your board should now have a photo background.

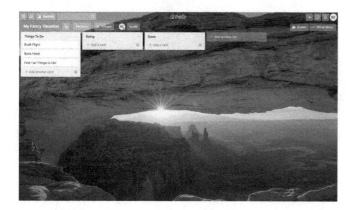

[2]

CRASH COURSE

This chapter will cover:
- Trello basics
- Search operators
- Board creation
- Trello templates

NAVIGATING TRELLO

Now that we know how to change our board background, let's learn basic navigation, then we'll see how to create boards, lists, and cards.

As you navigate around, you'll notice there's no Save button. Once you create it, it's saved and synced everywhere. So there's never a need to save.

Over on the upper left side are the three main navigation buttons.

The nine small squares will show you other Atlassian apps that you have connected to Trello (if any). The two most popular are Jira and Confluence. Trello is the most commercial of Atlassian's products—most of their tools have an enterprise feel and are better for larger businesses.

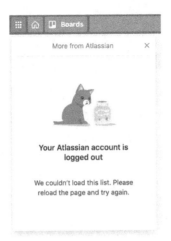

The Home button will take you to a dashboard interface with all of your boards.

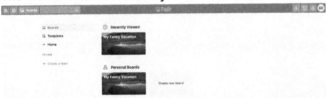

The Boards button will show you a drop-down of your boards and also let you search for boards by name, which comes in handy when you start creating lots of them.

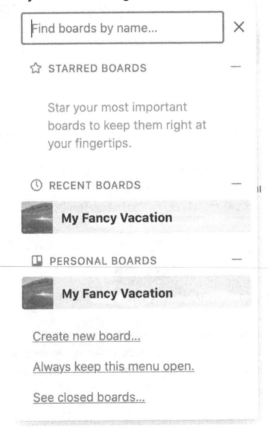

Over on the right side, the + button is where you can quickly create a board or create a team.

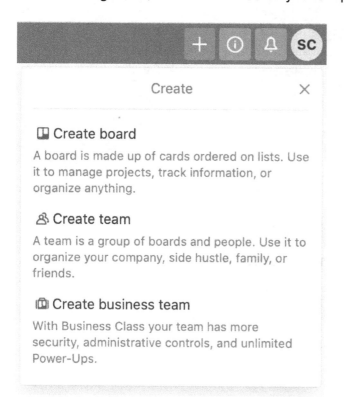

The circled "i" is the tips button; click that for little tips about using Trello.

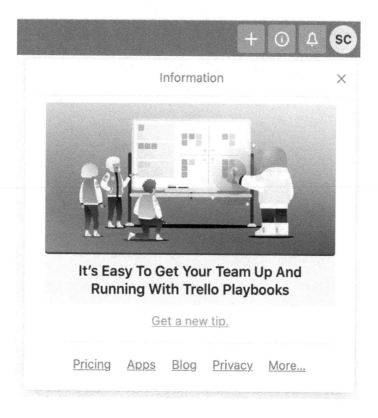

The bell button is for notifications (if any); you'll see a sleeping Taco (Trello's mascot) if you have no new notifications.

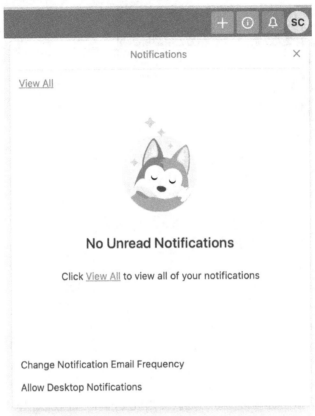

Finally, the last button is for your account settings, which we will cover later in this book.

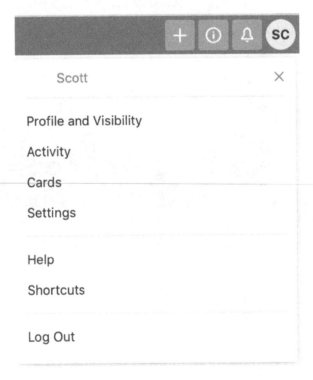

Next to boards is a search menu. Unlike the Board search, this searches everything on Trello. You can use the @ sign to search for cards and files created by specific people once you start adding them to your account.

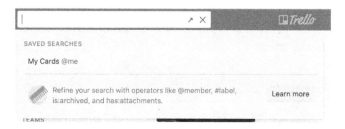

SEARCH OPERATORS

As you search Trello you can use different search commands called "operators." Below is a list of operators currently accepted in the search (and remember, you can combine operators to refine the search even more).

- "-" - Adding the minus (-) in front of a search will look for cards without that operator (for example, you can say -@team_member to search for cards that don't include that team member.
- @name - looks for cards with this specific team member.
- #label - When we get into creating cards, you'll see how you can add different labels to cards. To search those labels, just add a # and type the label.
- Board:id - search for cards only on a specific board.
- List:name - search for specific lists.
- Has:attachments - looks only for cards with attachments.
- Due:day - search for cards by a specific due day. You can also add due:week to see cards due that week; due:month to see cards due that month; and due:overdue to see anything that's late.
- Create:day - lets you search for when a card was created.
- Edited:day - lets you search for cards by when they were last edited.
- Description: - lets you search for what's in a specific aspect of a card; for example, you can say checklist:eggs to search for any cards that have a checklist and the checklist item is eggs.
- Is: - Is:open - searches all open cards; is:archive searches all archived closed; is:starred searches only cards you have starred.

CREATING BOARDS

There are two places to create a board in Trello. The quickest way to add a board is to click the + button in the upper right and click Create Board.

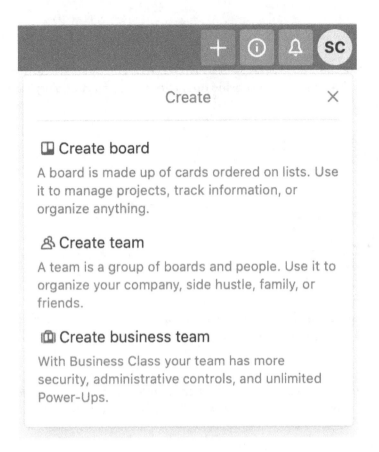

You can also create a board by clicking the Home button in the upper left, then clicking on the Create New Board next to your current board.

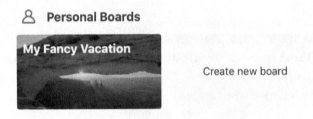

Once you click add a new board, there will be a very small pop-up.

To the right side, you can click the box with the three dots to change the board's background.

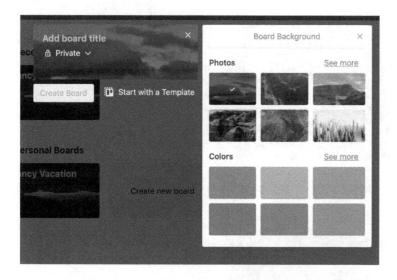

By default, the board is private; clicking on Private will open a drop-down and you can make the board public. A public board can be seen by anyone on the Internet (only you can change the content, but Trello boards do come up in Google searches if you make them Public).

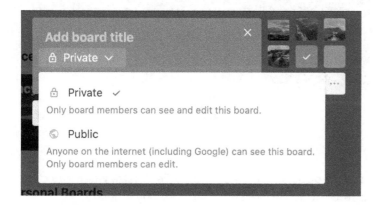

If you have teams, you can assign them to the board.

Once you give your board a name, the Create Board button will turn green and you can click it to create it.

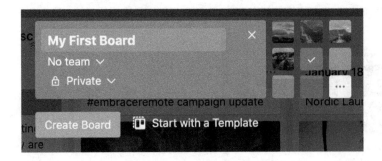

Your board is now created. It's completely blank at this point, so in the next section, we'll look at creating lists.

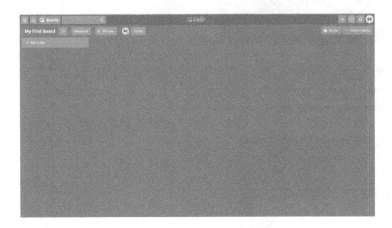

STARTING FROM A TEMPLATE

When you create a board, you'll also see an option called Start with a Template; when you click that, you'll see that Trello has dozens of boards already created for virtually any industry.

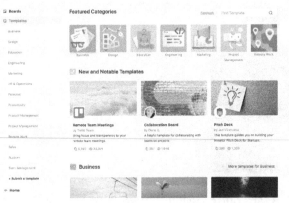

You can click on any template to read about what it is and see a little preview.

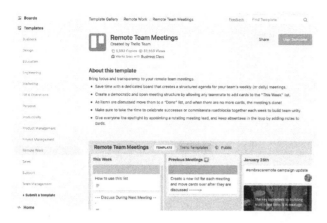

To use the template, click the green Use Template button. There are a couple of options before you add it—you can rename it, keep the cards and keep the template cards.

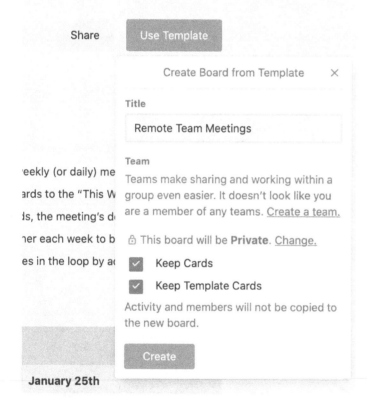

Once you click Create, you'll see the new board.

[3]
CREATING A LIST

This chapter will cover:
- Create a list
- Move a list
- Watch a list
- Archive a list

Now that you have your board, you are ready for your list. Just click the + Add a list to get started. Creating a list is very simple—add the title, click the green Add List and you are done.

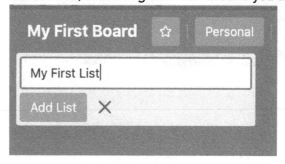

You can add an infinite number of lists by continuing to repeat the steps.

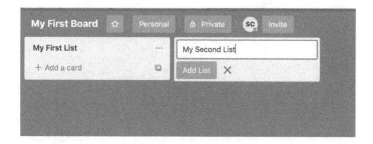

As you create more, you'll probably want to move them around. Just click and hold the list, then drag it wherever you want it to go.

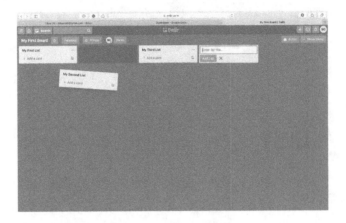

Each list has a subset of options that you can access by clicking on the three dots in the right corner of each list box.

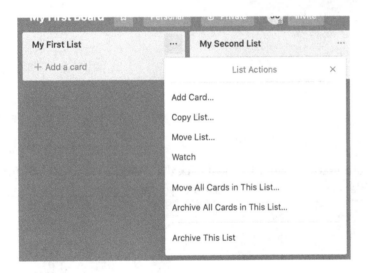

MOVE LIST

One of the more powerful options under lists options is the Move All Cards option. This lets you quickly move everything in a list to another list.

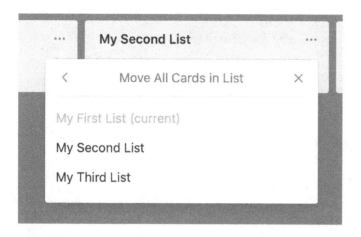

The Move List option takes it a step forward by letting you move the entire list to an entirely different board.

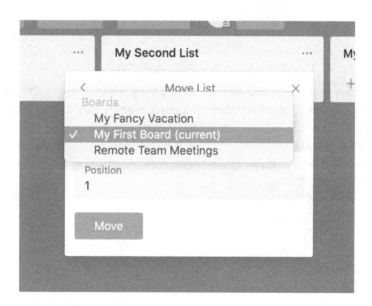

WATCH LIST

As your lists grow, you can click the Watch list icon to follow particular lists.

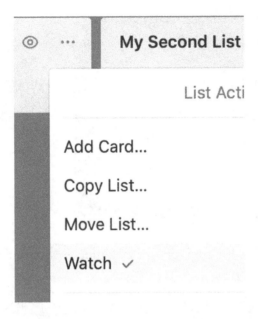

ARCHIVE LISTS

Archiving lists removes the lists and all the cards from your board, but they aren't completely deleted. It is basically hidden—removed from the board in an invisible area. You can still search for cards that were on it.

If you accidentally archive it, you can get it back by clicking on the Show Menu on the right side, then clicking the More option.

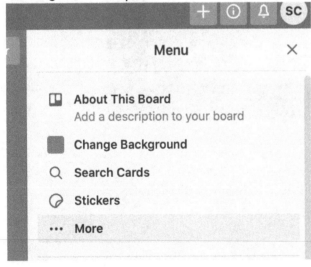

Under More, click Archived Items.

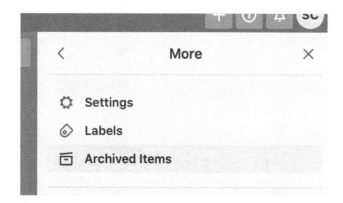

By default, this will show archived cards first; if you archived a list, click the Switch to Lists button.

Once you see what you are looking for, click the Send to Board.

[4]

CREATING A CARD

This chapter will cover:
- Create a card
- Power-ups
- Moving / copying cards
- Sharing cards
- Card activity
- Formatting cards
- Templates

Each list can have an infinite number of cards; these cards are kind of like projects within projects; your list might be something like Vacation and your cards would be all the things to make that vacation happen. To create a card, click the + Add a card option.

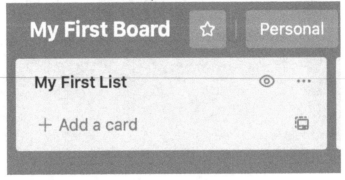

Once you title the card, you'll see the green Add card button can now be clicked.

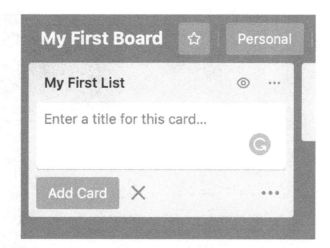

Next to the Add card button are three dots that represent more options; this lets you assign labels, member and a card position (the order it appears on the list) to the card before you add the card to your list.

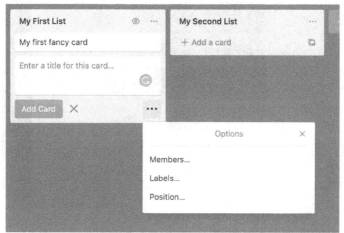

Once you add it, you can click the card one time to bring up an expanded list of options.

Clicking on any of the options will let you change something. For example, Labels lets you add labels or tags to the card.

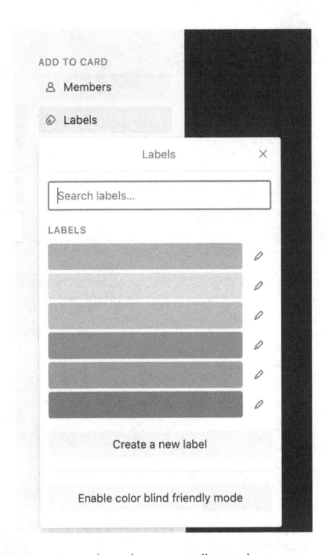

Due dates help you organize your cards so they eventually get done; you can set notifications to have reminders that a card is almost due.

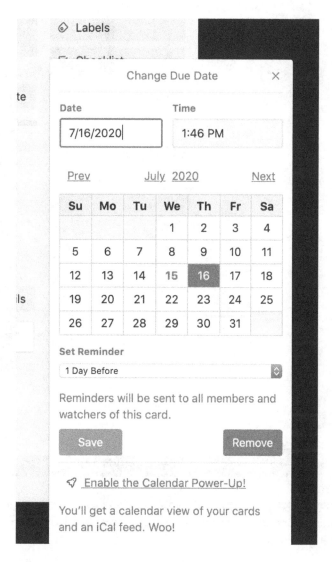

You can also attach files and links to a card. Trello integrates with most popular cloud storage solutions like Google Drive and Dropbox.

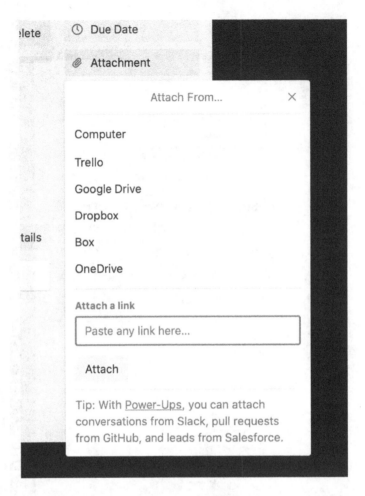

Just like you can have board backgrounds, you can also have card backgrounds. Images can get a little large on cards, and colors are much more practical. You can also attach a cover image (such as a gif if you want something animated).

CREATING A CARD CHECKLIST

A Checklist is a set of steps needed for the card to be complete. When you click this option, the first step is to name your checklist, then click Add.

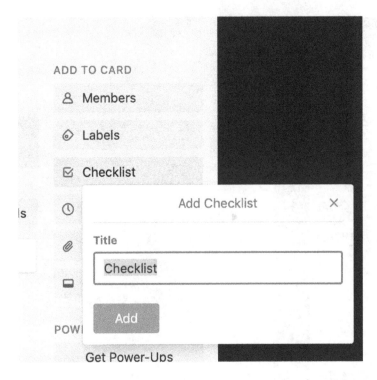

You can now start adding items to your checklist.

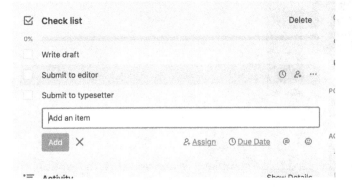

As you add items, you can assign them to people and also add due dates (you have to upgrade your Trello subscription to a paid plan for this option).

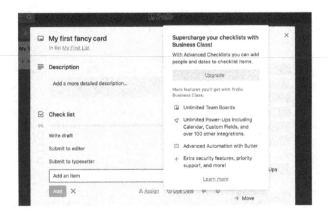

When a person checks off the item, you can monitor the progress. You can also hide completed items from showing or delete the list entirely by clicking the options above.

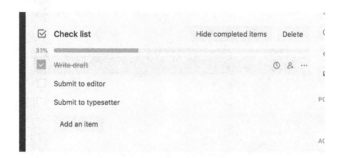

If you want to edit an item in a checklist, just click the title once.

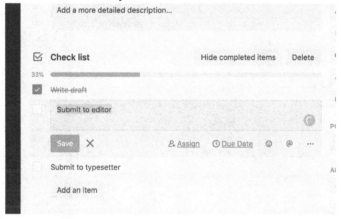

CARD POWER-UPS

Power-ups let you add integrations to your card. Power-ups are advanced (and often paid) integrations to help automate your cards or add other features.

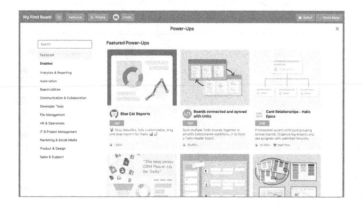

MOVING AND COPYING CARDS

Moving and copying cards works the same way it does with lists; you can move / copy cards to other lists or you can move / copy cards to other boards.

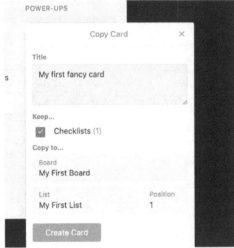

Sharing Cards

If you have another team member who is asking where your card is, there's an option at the bottom to share the card; click that, then grab the link to the card.

Archiving and Deleting Cards

Unlike lists, which you can only archive, cards you can delete. To do either, click the Archive button once. Once archives it (Send to board undoes it); once you click it once, the option to delete it will appear.

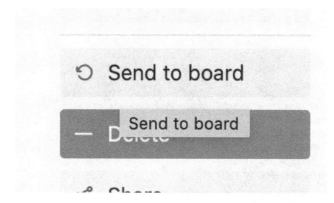

If you select Delete, it will remind you that the action cannot be undone.

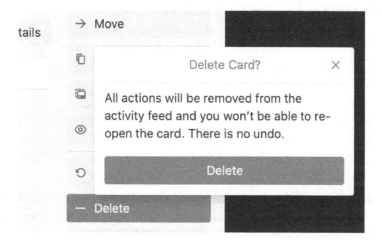

When a card is archived, you'll see a message on top of your card telling you; when it's deleted it disappears for good—no undo!

CARD ACTIVITY

At the bottom of the page, you can select Show Activity to see what actions people have performed on the card. If another team member has added something to the card or changed anything, you'll see it here.

FORMATTING HELP

The description at the top can have a very basic description.

Trello has its own formatting language, however, to make the description a little nicer; if you click Formatting Help, it will show you all the possible styles that you can add to the description.

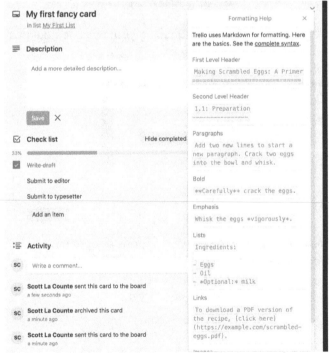

MOVING CARD

Once a card is created, you can click and drag it to any other list. The most common reason people do this is to move cards from a list for "doing" to a list for "done."

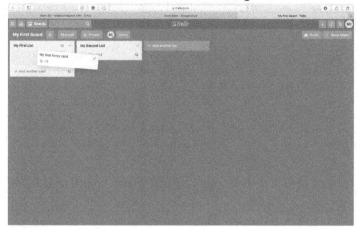

CREATE A TEMPLATE

You can also create a card from a Template. This creates a card that has preset things in place, so you don't have to repeat creating them. To get started, click the Template button to the right of + Add a card, then select Create a New Template.

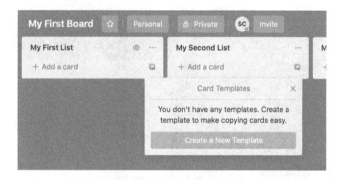

Once you add all the parameters, you are all set.

When you select that option again, you'll see the template card as an option. From here, you can click it to use it, or you can create a new template card or edit the previous template card.

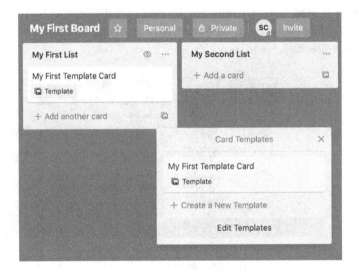

[5]

CREATING YOUR TEAM

This chapter will cover:
- Create a team
- Manage a team

Creating boards to get stuff done is nice, but Trello really shines when you work together with others. While the most obvious thing that will come to mind when you think of boards is business use, Trello can also be useful in your personal life. My wife and I have used Trello for household tasks to assign who does what and when it will get done—we both can create and assign tasks and due dates for each other and it all syncs together.

To create a team, click the + button in the upper right corner, and click Create team (You can also create a business team, which is the same thing as a team, but with more features unlocked—you have to pay for this type of team).

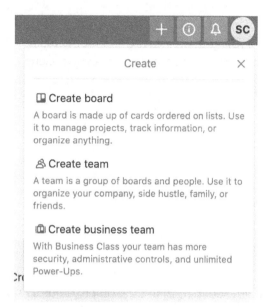

A pop-up will appear to build your first team. The first two fields are required, but you can make up any name you want. The last field (description) is not required.

Your team type is not that important; if nothing fits, then select "Other."

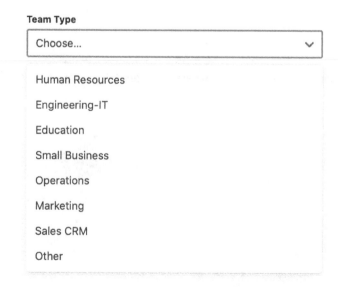

Once you have added everything, then select Continue. You'll now be able to invite people to your team, but you can also skip this part and add people later by clicking on the I'll do this later link at the bottom.

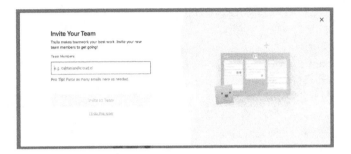

As you type in emails, you might see some show up with their names; that just means they are already a Trello user. If you don't see that, then the person needs to sign up for an account. You can add as many people as you like—you don't have to invite them one at a time—just keep adding emails until you are done. Each person (regardless if they are a Trello user) will get an email asking them to accept the invite.

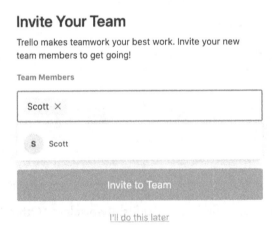

Once you invite everyone, you'll see your team dashboard. Right now it's empty because you haven't created any boards. If you have created boards, you have to assign them to your team (I'll show you how below).

At any point you can change the team's profile by clicking on Edit Team Profile. You can also give your team a logo / icon, by clicking on that icon of the two people.

If you did not invite anyone to your team (or you want to invite more), then click on the Members tab. Here, you can also remove people from the team.

The Settings tab lets you link your team to Slack, so you can collaborate on projects within your Slack channel; you can also change if the team is private or public. If you have a paid Trello account, you'll be able to set board restrictions and assign team roles (e.g. who are admins).

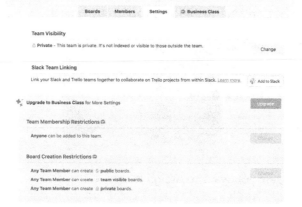

Unless you are a paid member, the Business Class tab will just be an ad to upgrade; if you pay for Trello this is where you can manage things like Power-ups.

When you close this dashboard, you can access it again by clicking on the Home button in the upper left of your screen. Before, this would be a dashboard for your boards; now, however, you will see your team has been added.

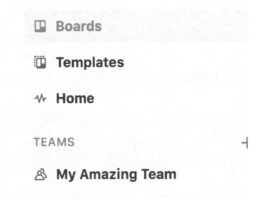

If you already have a board and want to assign it to a team, then go to the board you want to assign and click the Invite button near the middle top of the board.

You can now pick the team you want to assign it to.

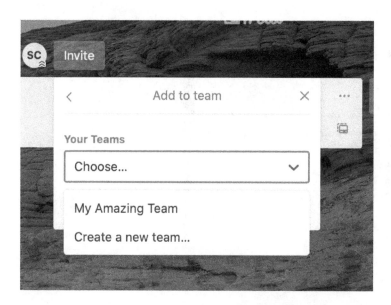

Once you click it, select Add to team.

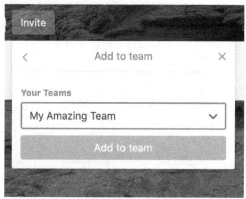

You can also invite people not on your team by creating a board link. Copy and send the link to anyone you want to see the board, and they'll have access.

When you click on your Home button again and go to your team page, you'll see that your board is now listed under your team.

[6]

THE BUTLER

This chapter will cover:
- What is the Butler
- Butler rules
- Card buttons
- Board buttons
- Due dates

You may have noticed a little button on the right side of your board called the Butler; this is where you can go to automate your boards and create commands to make your life easier.

RULES

There are several things in the Butler; the first is Rules. A rule is a little command that you create that says, "when this happens, then make this happen." To add a rule, click the Create Rule button.

Turn your Trello board into an automation machine.

The first thing you have to do is add a trigger (i.e. "when this happens").

There are all kinds of triggers you can add. In this example, my rule will be simple: when anyone in the team moves a card.

Next, I have to find my "make this happen." In this case, my "make this happen" will be the card will get a red label. Now whenever anyone in my team moves a card, I'll see a red label on it and can quickly identify that it has been moved.

CARD BUTTONS

Card buttons let you add custom buttons to your card. Click Create Button to get started.

Before you can pick what you want your button to do, give it an icon and name.

Next, select the button's action. In this example, the button will let members quickly subscribe to the card to monitor activity.

You can edit any of these custom actions (or delete them) by clicking on the thumbnail icons next to the customization.

BOARD BUTTONS

Just like cards, you can also create buttons for your entire board.

In this example, I created a board button that lets you sort a list on the board by the date each card was created.

When you leave the Butler area, you'll see that the button is now available on your board.

When you click the button, you'll see the Butler running the command on the bottom of your screen.

CALENDAR AND DUE DATE

The last two options are for paid Trello plans only. Calendar lets you set up commands based on recurring schedules.

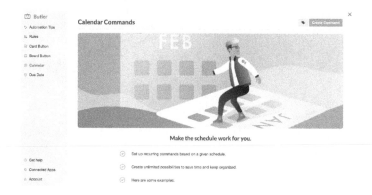

Due date helps you manage when your cards are due.

Due Date Commands

Never forget a due date.

Create commands based on a card's due date.

Stay on timeline and manage due dates on cards, stress-free

Here are some examples!

[7]
ACCOUNT SETTINGS

This chapter will cover:
- Account settings

Trello's account settings are unlike some account settings you are used to. They are simple! To get to your settings, click the round button with your initials in the upper right corner, then click Settings.

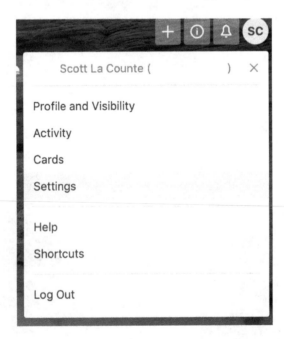

The settings are very straightforward and let you change notifications, your default language, and opt out of marking emails.

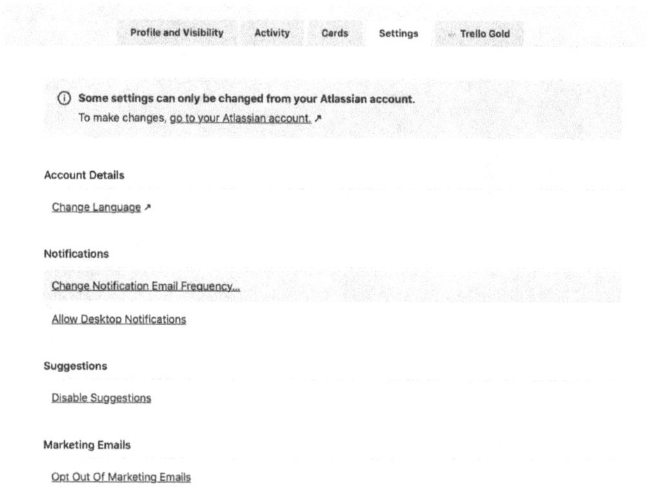

Profile and Visibility   Activity   Cards   Settings   — Trello Gold

(i) **Some settings can only be changed from your Atlassian account.**
To make changes, go to your Atlassian account. ↗

Account Details

Change Language ↗

Notifications

Change Notification Email Frequency...

Allow Desktop Notifications

Suggestions

Disable Suggestions

Marketing Emails

Opt Out Of Marketing Emails

INTRODUCTION

Chromebooks of the past used to be more of a novelty best suited for casual use. In 2013, Google tried to change this with the Chromebook Pixel—its first higher-end Chromebook. While most saw it as a worthy first effort, it was not largely viewed as ready for primetime.

Google discontinued its first official Chromebook in August of 2016 and announced its successor in October of 2017: The Pixelbook. Everything about the successor proved that Google had learned from previous generation Chromebooks and was ready to seriously compete with the Windows Surface and Macbook.

The hardware alone matched high-end Mac and Windows computers, but the software is where the Chromebook really shines. In addition to Google Assistant, a Siri-like tool for productivity, the computer also is amongst the first Chromebooks to be able to run Android apps—combined with a convertible touchscreen, this means you can leave your tablet at home. For a better comparison of how the computer ranks against Windows and Mac, see Appendix A.

Google isn't alone in its attempt to make Chromebooks a serious PC/Mac competitor. There are dozens like it—each with specifications that prove it is a novelty no more. Today it is used in businesses and schools alike to create major projects.

If you've used any computer, then a Chromebook will be easy enough to use as soon as you open it up for the first time. If you really want to take advantage of all the features and be as productive as possible, then this guide will help. Let's get started!

[1]

TELL ME THE BASICS AND KEEP IT RIDICULOUSLY SIMPLE

This chapter will cover:
- What's Chrome OS
- The Keyboard

A WORD (OR PARAGRAPH OR TWO) ABOUT CHROME OS

For years, Google has taken what you could call the "Apple approach" to computers and tablets. Computers ran Chrome and tablets ran Android (e.g. iPads run iOS and MacBooks run MacOS). Like iPads and Macbooks, there were similarities between Android tablets and Chrome computers. But there were also differences.

The Pixel Slate breaks this tradition by running the same operating system (OS) that you are familiar with if you have a Chromebook. What's more, newer Chromebooks can also download Android apps. That means if there's an app you love on your phone, you can use it on your computer as well.

THE KEYBOARD

The layout of the keyboard isn't completely different from other computers, but there are a few keys you might not be familiar with. The list below is an overview of those keys. Because there are so many different Chromebook models, this list will vary, so the following is just a reference.

●	Searches all the apps installed on your computer as well as the web. This button is where the Caps Lock key normally is—to use Caps Lock, hit this button and the Alt key at the same time.
●ᵢ	Launches the Google Assistant (Google's version of Siri).
←	Goes to the previous page in your browser history.
C	Reloads your current page.
[ ]	This puts your current application in full screen mode; all the tabs and the launcher will be hidden.

▢⫾	Shows all windows in Overview mode.
☼	Dim the screen. (F5)
☼	Make the screen brighter. (F6)
▶❙❙	Play/pause (F7)
🔇	Mute (F8)
🔉	Lower the volume. (F9)
🔊	Raise the volume. (F10)
☰	Open your status area (where your account picture appears).

[2]

ALL ABOUT CHROME OS

This chapter will cover:
- User accounts
- Settings overview

Chrome OS is a very close relative of Google's Internet browser, Google Chrome. As the owner of a Chromebook, you'll quickly see that Chrome is about to become a very big part of your life. This is a good thing; it's a fast, easy-to-use web browser with all kinds of features and seemingly unlimited potential for enhancement thanks to apps and extensions available in the Chrome Web Store. The Chrome browser means so much more than just web browsing in Chrome OS though, due to the fact that almost every app you run in Chrome OS runs inside a Chrome browser window. Don't worry if that sounds bizarre at first—you'll get the hang of it quickly and we'll walk you through everything you need to know!

The Chrome Web Store contains products that are similar enough to major desktop applications that you'll hardly be able to tell the difference. As a bonus, many of them are completely free (and if you've ever shelled out for Photoshop, we know that's going to come as a relief!).

Since most of Chromebook's functionality happens within a browser, Chromebook users can get to the majority of their Chromebook work from any computer with the free Google Chrome browser installed. Google's cloud storage system—Google Drive—is baked into Chrome OS and steadily saves your work as you go. As long as you're connected to wi-fi, if catastrophe strikes your physical Chromebook, your important files and documents are safe and sound in the cloud.

If you're scratching your head at this point, don't worry. Chromebook is easy to use, and the best way to understand it is to turn the thing on, roll up your sleeves, and dive right in. And we're going to do just that in the next chapter!

USER ACCOUNTS

One of the best features about any Chromebook is the ability to add user accounts; unlike other computers, you can take all of your settings with you. So let's say you have a Chromebook, and log in to another Chromebook. All of your apps, settings, customizations are there waiting for you. It's almost like you are using your personal computer even though you are logged in as a guest. This also means when you get another computer in the future, it's very simple to set up. Just log in and you are done!

Having multiple accounts also makes it very easy to share a computer in your household. From the login screen, you can either add a user or log in as a guest. Anyone who has a Google account (if you have Gmail then you have one—if you don't have Gmail you might have one without knowing it, as this is what many businesses use), can set up an account on your computer. Don't worry: this won't give other users access to any of your files or personal settings.

There is only one important thing to remember with regard to user accounts: set up the device owner first! If you use another account to sign into the computer for the first time, then that's the device owner and the person who will have administrator rights that other users won't have. There's no way to transfer ownership to another user, so you would have to reset your computer if that happens.

SETTINGS OVERVIEW

We'll discuss the settings a little further throughout this book, but there are a few settings you'll want to know about right now.

User Accounts

If you want to disable people from being able to log in to your settings, then log in to your account, click on your user profile image (bottom right corner of the screen), then click the settings button:

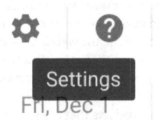

From here, you'll be taken to a browser window with a list of some of the most common settings. Scroll to the bottom of the list and click the button labeled "Manage Other Users." By default, everything is toggled on; click it once to toggle it off. Hit the back button and it saves your settings automatically.

Keyboard Settings

The location of the Alt key on a computer keyboard is what a Mac user might use as the Command key. There are several keys like this. You can either retrain your mind or you can go into the keyboard settings and change the shortcuts around a little. In the settings you can also change things like the language.

Touchpad Settings

Mac users will be a little annoyed with scrolling on their new computer! That's because the scrolling on an Apple device is the opposite of scrolling on the Chromebook! Again, you can either retrain your mind or you can just change the setting. "Australian" is the scrolling you will want. Another setting you will probably want to change is the Touchpad speed; to some users, it might feel a little laggy. It's an easy fix. Just slide the Touchpad speed button to the right for a faster scroll.

[3]

GETTING AROUND THE OS

This chapter will cover:
- The Desktop
- Launcher and Chrome Shelf
- Chrome Windows
- Files and Google Drive
- Offline Mode

Google's OS seems much like a marriage between Windows OS and Mac OS, and that's a good thing, because with very little instruction, everything will start feeling natural. In this section, you'll get a crash course in the basic features of the OS and where things are located.

DESKTOP

Your desktop takes up the bulk of the screen. It includes a desktop wallpaper image, which can be customized, and you can also store files and shortcuts here for easy access, just like other desktops. Chances are, however, you'll probably find yourself not making much use of the Desktop space. Chrome's intuitive interface makes it easier just to store everything in your Google Drive. I've used Chrome OS for many years, and I find the desktop is usually just a place to put a pretty picture.

THE LAUNCHER AND CHROME SHELF

The Launcher button is similar to the Start button on a Windows computer—only a bit simpler. Clicking on the Launcher button will reveal every app associated with your Google account. This apps menu does extend to the right, and you may need to use the horizontal page indicator icons at the bottom of the menu to move from screen to screen.

Next to the Apps button, you'll find your Chrome "shelf." You might be used to thinking of this area as a taskbar or dock, but in Chrome, it's called the shelf. The shelf contains shortcuts to your favorite apps and documents, and lets you know what's currently running. In the screenshot above, you can see that we're currently running the Chrome browser, gmail, the app HipChat, and the Files app, due to the small gray dot under those icons.

To the far right (where your photo is) is the Systems Tray Menu; this is where you'll see settings, apps that have updated, and battery life.

CHROME WINDOWS

Chrome is almost entirely browser based; there are a few more traditional looking apps (like Google Hangouts), but most of the apps you see on your Chrome Shelf are more like shortcuts to a web page. I'll explain the apps that come with the Chromebook and how to get additional ones later in this book.

FILES AND GOOGLE DRIVE

Every computer has "local" storage—which is all the stuff (files, photos, documents) that are stored directly on the computer; Windows computers have File/System Explorer; Mac Computers have Finder; and Chrome computers have Files. Chrome computers have one extra storage drive: Google Drive. Google Drive is cloud-based, which means whatever you store there will be available on the Internet (privately unless you make it public). This makes it easy to store a file that you want to use on another computer. The Files app shows you both local files (on your computer) and cloud files (stored online). If you were to connect a USB storage device like a flash drive or an external hard drive, you'd see that in Files as well.

Keep in mind that Google Drive is not unlimited storage; your Google account has 15GB of free storage. After that, it's $1.99 a month and up. It's a very inexpensive solution, and one you should consider for backing up files you store on your computer. Also, buying any new Chromebook may mean you are qualified for free storage. You can see Google's current offerings here: https://www.google.com/chromebook/offers/

OFFLINE

The Chromebook is designed to be used online. That said, the Internet is not required. Even Google's suite of online apps (Docs, Sheets, and Slides) can be used offline. If you plan to work on a Google Doc file (or Sheets/Slides) make sure you move it into the offline folder before logging off.

[4]

ALL ABOUT CHROME OS

This chapter will cover:
- Anatomy of the Chrome Window
- Tabs and Windows
- Incognito
- Bookmarks
- History
- Passwords
- Autofill
- Chrome Extensions
- Web Store and Apps
- Installing and Managing Chrome Content

THE CHROME BROWSER

The web browser that comes standard with your Chromebook is, for all intents and purposes, the very same version of Chrome that's available for Windows, OSX, and Linux computers. So if you're already using Chrome on another device, then there's very little learning curve. One thing you'll love right away is all of your bookmarks and settings will be carried over from one device to the next. There are still a few things you'll want to know about, so I'll cover them here.

You'll notice that opening Chrome doesn't automatically put the browser into full-screen mode. You can resize Chrome window two different ways—by pressing the green maximize button or by tapping the three dots in the top right corner and then tapping the full-screen button next to the zoom options.

If you're using Chrome on other devices, you'll be able to access all of your currently open pages and bookmarks by clicking "Other Devices," (click the three dots, hover over "history," and scroll to the bottom of the list). If you've accidentally closed a web page, Chrome will save it for a period of time under the "Recently Closed" menu.

ANATOMY OF A GOOGLE CHROME WINDOW

Chrome stays out of your way, for the most part. The vast majority of a Chrome window is reserved for content—whether it's a web page, a Google Docs document, a game, or any other Chrome app.

Everything you need to manage a Chrome window is located at the top of the page. At the top right corner, you'll see the Back, Forward and Refresh buttons. These are used to navigate back or forward through your recent screen views and to reload a page. They match up with the three keys on the keyboard directly to the right of the ESC key on the top row.

In the center of the top part of the screen, you'll see the address/search bar, known as the Chrome "omnibox." Type a website's address (google.com, facebook.com) here to go directly to that site. You can also use this area as a search bar ("kittens," "DIY birdhouse," etc.).

At the right end of the omnibox, you'll see a star. Click that star to bookmark the web page (we'll go into more detail on this process in just a second).

Finally, at the far top right corner, you'll see the Chrome menu button. Here you'll find everything else you need to manage a Chrome window. We'll refer to this button pretty often throughout this guide!

TABS AND WINDOWS

There are two viewing units to be aware of in Chrome—tabs and windows. Tabs open inside one window, as pictured below. You can open a new tab by pressing CTRL+T (remember: t for tab), by right-clicking the Chrome icon in the shelf, or by clicking ≡ > New Tab.

Opening a page in a new window, on the other hand, opens a completely separate frame (which can then be populated with a new group of tabs, if you like). You can open new windows by pressing

CTRL+N (N for new), by right-clicking the Chrome icon on the shelf, or by clicking  > New Window.

When tabs were first introduced, they streamlined the laborious process of switching between several windows while browsing the Internet. As a result, many users now associate tabs with easier workflow. However, on a Chromebook, it's often easier to switch between windows than between tabs, thanks to the Window Switch key on the top row. Pressing the Window Switch key reveals every open window, giving you the title and a visual preview of each one. Keep this in mind when you're formulating your workflow windows/tabs strategy!

BROWSING INCOGNITO

If you're shopping for birthday presents, or doing anything else that you don't want enshrined in your search history, Incognito is the browsing mode for you. Pages you view while in an Incognito tab won't be saved in your history. Search terms won't resurface in your search history, and website cookies won't be stored on your computer. However, if you download or bookmark anything, remember that it will be retained on your system.

To open an Incognito tab in Chrome, press CTRL+SHIFT+N, right-click the Chrome icon on the shelf, or click 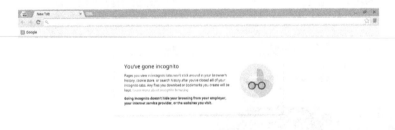 > New Window. You can tell at a glance which windows are Incognito by looking for the shadowy figure in sunglasses peeking from behind the top left corner.

BOOKMARKS

Bookmarks are a handy way to organize your favorite sites for fast access later on. There are a few different ways to bookmark a site. You can click the Star outline in the omnibox, as previously

discussed, or you can press CTRL+D. You can also navigate to  > Bookmarks > Bookmark this page.

By default, your bookmarks are stored in the bookmarks bar, which is not visible by default. The bookmarks bar, when enabled, appears underneath the omnibox. To display the bookmarks bar, click

> Bookmarks > Show bookmarks bar, or press CTRL+SHIFT+B. To hide it, follow the same path or use the same keyboard shortcut.

If you don't like the automatic wording for each bookmark, you can easily edit it, either when adding the bookmark or later by managing your bookmarks. To manage bookmarks, right-click the

bookmark and then click Edit (or Delete, or whatever you need to do). Then click > Bookmarks > Bookmark Manager, or press CTRL+SHIFT+O. Inside the bookmark manager, you can right-click bookmarks to edit them, as pictured below. You can also rearrange the order of your bookmarks either in the Bookmark Manager or by dragging them around on the bookmarks bar itself. The most common edit we make for bookmarks is shortening the name in order to fit as many as possible in our bookmarks bar!

Of course, you may eventually run out of room in the bookmarks bar. If this happens, a double arrow will appear at the end of the bookmark bar. Clicking the arrow will reveal the rest of your bookmarks. This may be enough for you, but if you'd like a better way of managing large numbers of bookmarks, we recommend organizing your bookmarks into folders. To do this, open the Bookmark Manager (CTRL+SHIFT+O). Click the Folders heading on the left, and then click Add folder.

You can add as many folders as you like. Once the folders are added, you can drag your bookmarks into them in the Bookmarks Manager. You can either display your folders on the

bookmarks bar or organize them in the Other Bookmarks folder, which you can get to at  >
Bookmarks.

Don't forget that in Chrome OS, practically everything you look at is going to be a web page. This means that you can set up bookmarks for Google Docs documents, Google Slides presentations, games, etc. It's a great way to organize a project as well as a way to organize your favorite websites.

RECENT AND HISTORY

Chrome stores your recently viewed pages and full browsing history to make it easy to get back to

places you've already been. You can see your recently closed tabs at   > Recent. This is a lifesaver if you accidentally close a tab!

You'll find your full browsing history at   > History or by pressing CTRL+H (H for history). To clear your history at any time, visit your History and then click Clear browsing data. You can either delete history from the past hour, day, week, month, or, as Google so poetically phrases it, the beginning of time. You can also specify what kind of history you want to delete. For example, you can delete your list of recently visited sites, but retain any passwords you've saved in Chrome.

GOOGLE CHROME AND YOUR GOOGLE ACCOUNT

When you set up a new Chromebook, your system will automatically sign you in to the Google Chrome browser. You can sign into Chrome from other computers as well, though. Signing in to Chrome will allow you to see your browsing history from other Chrome sessions on other computers, your stored passwords, your extensions, and more. To sign into Chrome, click Sign in at the top right corner of a Chrome browser window.

STORED PASSWORDS

Google Chrome will offer to remember passwords for you whenever you enter them into a website. A popup box will ask you if you want to save the password. You can say Nope to dismiss the box once, or you can click the arrow next to Nope for the Never for this site option.

Any passwords you save on your Chromebook or Slate will actually be associated with your Google account. This means that you can use them any time you sign into Chrome, on any computer (though we recommend avoiding signing in on public computers, just to be safe).

If you need to manage your stored passwords, visit ☰ > Settings. At the bottom of the Settings screen, click Show advanced settings. Scroll down until you see the Passwords and Forms heading. Underneath it, click Manage passwords. Here, you can edit or delete your stored passwords. You can also deselect Offer to save your web passwords if you don't want Chrome to store any passwords for you.

Passwords and forms

☑ Enable Autofill to fill out web forms in a single click. Manage Autofill settings

☑ Offer to save your web passwords. Manage passwords

FORM AUTOFILL

Form Autofill handles forms that you repeatedly fill in. It can remember your name, address, phone number, email address, etc. It's useful for repeated data entry, but you may occasionally need to manage your Autofill settings if you move or change your phone number. To do so, visit Settings > Passwords and forms and click Manage Autofill settings.

CHROME EXTENSIONS

Extensions extend Chrome's functionality in all kinds of ways, and the enormous range of free extensions to choose from is a huge part of what makes Google Chrome so great. We'll share some of our favorites later in Part 5, and you can explore on your own in the Web Store, which we'll cover next.

THE CHROME WEB STORE

You'll want to get to know the Web Store sooner rather than later, since it's where you'll find new apps and extensions for your Chromebook. Fortunately, this "Store" has an enormous free section in it, so tricking out your Chromebook won't necessarily break the bank!

You'll find the Web Store by clicking the Apps button in the lower left corner. If you're an Android user, be aware that the Chrome Web Store isn't exactly the same thing as the Google Play Store, though there's a lot of duplicated content.

There are three big categories in the Store—apps, extensions, and themes. You can choose which broad category you're interested in at the top of the Web Store navigation panel on the left.

Before jumping in, it's worth noting here a very big feature added to both the Chromebook and all new Chromebooks: The Android store!

Why is that important? All those apps that you've already downloaded on your Android tablet or phone can now be downloaded on your computer. It also turns your Chromebook into a tablet. You can download any app from the Play Store and it will install on your computer (play.google.com).

APPS

The apps section of the store contains two types of apps—Chrome apps and website apps. Website "apps" are basically bookmarks. These are websites that you can visit anywhere from any computer, generally with any browser. They're usually free. Chrome apps, on the other hand, make modifications to your Chrome browser in order to function. You will need to be running Chrome in order to use them, and they will need to be installed on the copy of Chrome you're using. This distinction is largely academic for most users. Whether an app is a web app or a Chrome app, adding it to your Chromebook will mean that it appears in your Apps button menu and that it can be pinned to your shelf.

Store apps can be browsed by category, using the dropdown menu under Categories in the left menu. You can also search by feature, like "runs offline" (meaning that the app doesn't require an Internet connection to function), by Google, Free, and Available for Android (very useful if you want to keep your Chromebook and Android smartphone or tablet closely in sync). Finally, you can also sort by the average star rating.

EXTENSIONS

Unlike apps, extensions allow you to do more with every page you visit in Chrome. Extensions let you do more with the Chrome browser, and there are all kinds of possibilities out there. There are extensions that convert currency on webpages for you, help you pin images to your Pinterest boards, generate secure passwords, or help you manage your online privacy.

Like apps, extensions can be narrowed down by category, special features (including Free), and star rating.

THEMES

Themes are similar to desktop wallpaper, but instead of decorating your desktop, they decorate the Chrome window itself. Themes change the appearance of an empty window, typically by showing an image or pattern, and altering the color of the outer edges of the window. In the example below, we've enabled a dark theme.

We freely admit that while apps and extensions make us salivate, we're not quite as enamored with Chrome theming. We're usually in too much of a hurry to get to our websites, content, and apps to appreciate them. Your mileage may vary, though, and it's not a bad idea to browse some of the free themes in the Store to see if any strike your fancy.

INSTALLING NEW CHROME CONTENT

Installing a new app, extension, or theme is incredibly simple, especially if it's free. To install free content, simply click the FREE text from a search result, and then click the Add to Chrome button that appears on the content's information screen.

If an app, extension, or theme costs money, click the Buy for... button.

Then click Add. At this point, if you haven't already set up Google Wallet, you'll be prompted to do so. Google Wallet is simply Google's credit card manager. Add a payment method as prompted, and Google will save that information for later. You can add more than one payment method if you prefer. From there, confirm the purchase, and your new paid app, extension, or theme will be installed for you.

MANAGING APPS, EXTENSIONS AND THEMES

After you've started amassing a library of apps, extensions and themes, you may occasionally need to temporarily disable or delete them. You can manage your apps by clicking the Apps button and then right-clicking the app you'd like to delete or alter.

Extensions are a little more complicated. You can find your extensions under ☰ > More Tools > Extensions, or under ☰ > History (alternately, press CTRL+H). On the History screen, click Extensions on the left. This will display a list of every installed extension on your system.

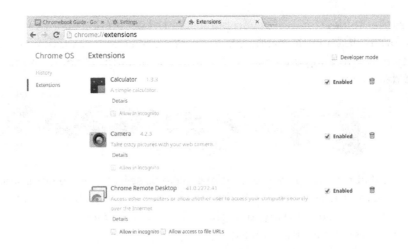

Note that you can disable extensions by deselecting the Enabled checkbox (a good temporary measure), or you can click the trashcan icon to permanently delete something.

[5]

There's a Pre-Installed App for That

This chapter will cover:
- Google Docs, Sheets, Slides
- Scratchpad
- Google+ Hangouts
- Gmail
- YouTube
- Calculator
- Camera
- Chrome Remote Desktop
- Photos
- Keep
- Google Maps and Google My Maps
- Google Forms
- Drawings
- Play Music, Play Books, and Play Movies
- Google Calendar
- Google Play
-

Just like any computer, your Chromebook will have apps installed right out of the box. Here is an overview and what they're good for.

GOOGLE DOCS

Google Docs, briefly, is Google's version of Microsoft Word or Apple Pages. You can edit a document just like you would in any other processor, but it's all online and synced automatically, which means it's very difficult to lose anything. You can also share documents and collaborate in real time.

Docs really shines through its connection to Google Drive. Anything you start in Google Docs is automatically saved in your Google Drive account—no need to worry about losing work through power failures, device catastrophes, or really just about any other scenario. Changes are saved as you go, and so are versions, so it's easy to revert to an earlier stage of a draft if you need to.

The main Docs menu consists of File, Edit, Insert, Format, Tools, Table, Add-ons, and Help. Each of these menu items contains a dropdown menu full of features. The full power of Docs is beyond the scope of this guide, but we'll show you some of the basics.

Starting a New Google Doc

To start a new document, simply open Docs for the first time, or click File > New to open a new document. Notice that Google Docs > File > New will also let you start new Sheets, Slides, Drawings, or Forms projects as well.

Saving a Google Doc

Google Docs saves everything as you go so you'll rarely need to save manually. You can find the status of your file to the right of the menu if you're concerned. Google Docs does save your work offline as well, so if you're not connected to Drive, you won't lose your work and you can verify that Chromebook has saved it for you.

All changes saved in Drive

All changes saved offline

Formatting a Google Doc

You'll find all the standard text editing options you'd expect in the top menu area, including font size, typeface, bold, italic, underline, text color, hyperlinks, and text alignment. If that doesn't cover you, though, you'll also find spacing, lists, indent control, and format clearing under More.

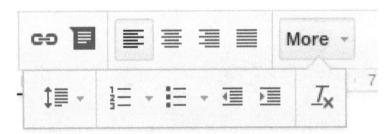

Collaborating Using Google Docs

Google Docs is hands-down one of the easiest ways to work on a group document. To invite people to share your Doc, click the blue Share button in the top right corner (note that hovering over this button will also give you the current shared status of your Doc).

You can add existing Google contacts by entering their names, or you can invite anyone through their email address. Note that your collaborators will need to set up a free Google Account to use Google Drive. You can choose the level of access you want collaborators to have—they can edit, comment, or merely view your shared document. You can remove them at any time by using the Share button again.

When two or more people are editing a document at the same time, you'll be able to see that person's cursor position and watch edits in real time. If you're concerned about losing work, remember that Google Docs saves version history for you, so it's easy to revert if you need to. Click File > See revision history (or press CTRL+ALT+SHIFT+G). By default, revisions are shown grouped into daily periods, but if you want to see changes made by the minute, click "Show more detailed revisions" at the bottom of the revisions panel. You can see which collaborator made each change in a group document. Of course, the slightly less elegant Undo and Redo functions are always available as well!

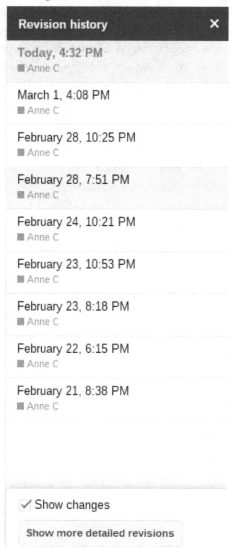

Dealing with Other File Formats

Fortunately, you can edit Microsoft Office files in Google apps like Google Docs. Just open the file and edit away. Google Docs can also open files with .ODT, .DOT, .HTML, and .TXT file extensions, though there's always a chance that the original formatting may not survive the conversion entirely intact.

Add-ons

Most of the Google productivity apps include the ability to add on functionality, typically designed by third party developers. You can search for add-ons by clicking the Add-ons menu item at the top of the screen. Click Get add-ons to start searching for the additional functions you need. For example, in Docs, you can install add-ons that reveal the document's structure in a table of contents presentation in the sidebar. There's even a Sudoku add-on for Sheets!

GOOGLE SHEETS

Google Sheets is Google's answer to Microsoft Excel. If you're familiar with any spreadsheet program, you should feel pretty at home in Sheets. Like almost every other spreadsheet program, Google Sheets will do all the heavy lifting for you when it comes to calculations. Entering formulas in Google Sheets is reasonably similar to Excel. Just type = at the beginning of a cell and then fill in your formula. Of course, there are some minor syntactical differences you'll need to get the hang of, but it's nothing too difficult. Sheets will help you build your formulas by giving you input examples, and you can create charts from your data and define custom sorting and filtering rules.

GOOGLE SLIDES

Google Slides is a presentation app, like Microsoft PowerPoint. Slides includes several prepackaged presentation themes to get you started, or you can begin with a blank slate. Your completed presentation can be downloaded as a PowerPoint, PDF, image, scalable vector graphic or plain text file, making Slides presentations compatible with just about any environment. There's also a very useful "Publish to the web" feature available in the File menu that will generate a public URL that you can share with your colleagues and/or the entire world. You can also embed Slides presentations in web pages or blog posts. To do this go to File and Publish to the Web.

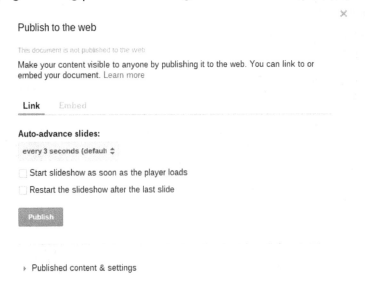

SCRATCHPAD

Scratchpad is meant for small, simple document creation (like Notes on Mac or Notepad on Windows). Things like grocery and to-do lists that don't necessarily need advanced formatting or structure for later publishing work well with Scratchpad.

GOOGLE+ AND HANGOUTS

Google+ began life as Google's attempt at a social network. It was their answer to Facebook and Twitter. If you are reading this wondering what is Google+ then you probably can tell they didn't quite accomplish everything they hoped. It will, in fact, be discontinued shortly.

Google+ has been out for over six years, which may surprise you. It certainly isn't Google's most widely used product, but it has grown in popularity since it came out and has evolved a lot. Sharing photos, videos, and more are made possible through the network. For businesses, the most important feature is Hangouts—a Skype-like service that lets you have group video calls and share screens.

To sign up for Google+, you'll first need to enter your name, gender, and birthday. Next, Google+ will suggest people you may know, based on any existing Gmail contacts you've entered. Use the Add button to add them to your circles (in Google+ you'll organize your contacts into circles, like friends, college buddies, frenemies, etc.).

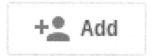

Next, Google+ will suggest some topics for you to follow that you might be interested in. Finally, you'll be able to update your profile by adding a photo and some additional personal details. Then you'll be all set to start using Google+!

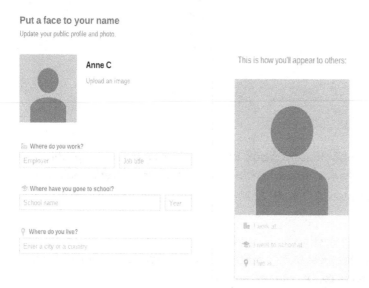

Inside the Google+ app, there are a few things to be aware of. In the top left corner, you'll see a button labeled Home. Click this button to expand the Google+ menu.

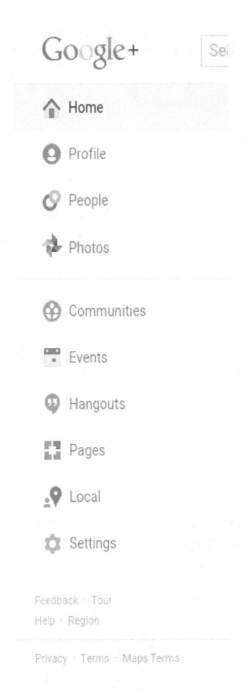

This menu should be familiar to Facebook users. You'll see options to get to your profile and edit it if necessary, as well as links to the people you follow and the photos you've posted. You'll also find Communities, Events, Hangouts, Pages, Local info, and Settings.

Posting in Google+

You can post various items in Google+, just like Facebook. You can add text, photos, links, videos, events (which you can invite your contacts to, of course), and polls.

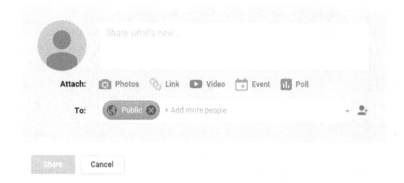

Google+ posts can be shared publicly, with certain people, or Google+ circles using the To: field in the post dialog box.

Hangouts

Without a doubt, Hangouts is the most successful aspect of Google+. It's like everything that was great about a late 1990s chat room combined with the power of Skype-like services. A Hangout generates a URL. Participants can use that link to leave and come back to a Hangout at any time, just like a chat room.

You can start a Hangout from inside Google+ or Gmail, or you can use the dedicated Hangouts app. To start a Hangout, you'll enter friends' names (if they're contacts in Google+) or email addresses (if they're not). You can also add entire Google+ circles or make a Hangout open to the entire public. If you'd rather have a private call, though, just add a single name.

Hangouts takes advantage of your Chromebook's built-in microphone and camera, just like Skype or FaceTime. It's easy to use and, as long as you have a free wi-fi connection, completely free.

GMAIL

Gmail is Google's proprietary email client, and we think it's the best of the bunch when it comes to web email hosts. If you've set up a new Google account for your Chromebook, then your Gmail address is your username plus @gmail.com. If you need to check your Gmail account from another computer, visit gmail.com and enter your Google Account username and password to sign in. You can open Gmail in any browser, like Internet Explorer or Firefox.

Opening the Gmail app on your Chromebook will take you straight to your Gmail inbox.

Gmail presorts your mail into three tabs—Primary, Social, and Promotions. This is a great way to tame an unruly inbox. All your Facebook notifications show up under Social, and those daily emails from that store you went to once will appear under Promotions, helping you focus on the email you most likely really want to read.

Of course, occasional mistakes will happen. If a message appears under the wrong tab, just drag it to the tab that you'd like future messages from that sender to appear under.

You'll notice the first time you open Gmail that the Chromebook Gmail app guides you through some basic setup tasks that will help you really get to know Gmail, if you don't already. You can choose a theme, import contacts, work through a tutorial, install Gmail on a mobile phone, and add a new profile image. Take some time and work through these steps—you'll be glad you did and it makes for a great introduction to Gmail.

Sending Email in Gmail

To start a new email message, open Gmail and click the red Compose button in the left menu.

This brings up the Compose pop-up screen, which allows you to compose your email while keeping an eye on your inbox. Enter the email address of your recipient in the To field and the subject of your email in the Subject field. If you need to add a CC (Carbon Copy, which is visible to other recipients) or BCC (Blind Carbon Copy—invisible to other recipients) recipient, click the gray Cc Bcc text in the top right corner of the New Message window. Then, of course, your message goes in the big blank area. When you're finished writing, click the blue Send button in the lower left corner of the New Message window to send your email.

Gmail also makes it easy to format your email and add attachments and multimedia. Next to the Send button, the A icon will display options for formatting text (bold, italics, font choice, etc.). Next, the paper clip icon opens up a dialog box that lets you browse your Chromebook for files to attach to your message, like PDFs, Google Docs documents, etc. If you have a file in Drive that you'd like to insert, use the Drive icon instead of the paper clip. You can use the $ icon as a sort of Google version of PayPal, if you have a credit card or bank account set up in your Google account. The camera icon lets you add images to your email—either as attachments or inside the email itself. Next, the chain link icon lets you add links to your email. If you type a full website address, like www.google.com, Gmail will recognize the link and will send it as such Finally, you can insert Google emoticons using the smiley face icon.

Gmail saves draft messages for you automatically. If you accidentally close a message you're working on, you'll find it safe and sound in your Drafts folder on the left. However, if you decide you don't want to save a draft message, use the trashcan icon in the lower right corner of the New Message window to delete it.

Inbox (3)

Starred

Sent Mail

Drafts

More ▾

The downward arrow in the far lower right corner of the New Message window gives you a few more options for managing your message. Perhaps the most immediately useful thing here is the spell-check function, but it's good to know how to print a draft or send it to full screen as well. We'll talk about labels in just a minute.

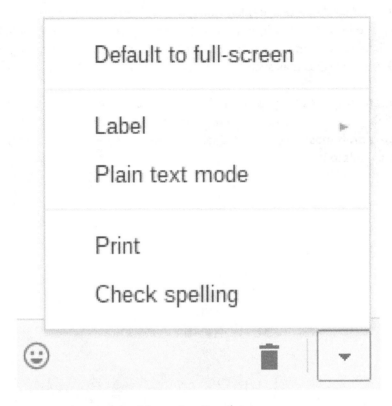

Managing Email

Gmail makes it exceptionally easy to deal with the daily barrage of incoming messages in this day and age. The toolbar pictured below appears at the top of every email, and will appear when emails are selected in the inbox or a folder.

When you're finished with a message, you can delete it, either from inside the opened message or by clicking the checkbox next to the email in your inbox, and then clicking the trashcan icon. However, Gmail makes it easy to get messages out of your inbox, thus decreasing clutter, without actually deleting them, thanks to its Archive feature. The archive button is the first icon in the Gmail toolbar. When you archive a message, it disappears from your inbox, but not from your account. You can search for it at any time using Gmail's search bar at the top of the Gmail screen.

Of course, sometimes archiving isn't quite nuanced enough, and that's where favorites and labels come in. To make an email a favorite, just click the star icon next to it. You can then get to all of your starred emails by clicking Starred in the left menu.

Labels are an easy way to categorize your email. You can add as many custom labels as you like in the left menu. Just click More in the left menu, and then click Create New Label at the bottom.

COMPOSE

Sent Mail

Drafts

Less ▲

Important

Chats

All Mail

Spam

Trash

▼ Categories

👥 **Social (1)**

🏷 Promotions

ⓘ Updates

💬 Forums

Manage labels

Create new label

To apply a label (or labels) to a message, click the Label icon in the top toolbar. A dropdown menu will appear that gives you a list of all of your existing labels. Click on one to apply it, or type in a new label in the box to set it up and add it to the message.

Contacts

You may have noticed that there's no dedicated contact app in Chromebook. That's because, between Gmail and Google+, there's no real need for one. Gmail is an excellent contacts manager in its own right, and Google+ adds additional contacts capabilities.

To manage contacts in Gmail, click the red Gmail text in the top left corner. A dropdown menu will appear, allowing you to switch to Contacts or Tasks view. All of your Google+ contacts will be automatically added, but you can add non-Google+ information and people as well. To manually add a new contact, click the red New Contact button.

NEW CONTACT

You can then add names, pictures, emails, phone numbers, addresses—basically, as much or as little information as you want. To add a field other than the ones displayed, just click the Add button underneath all of the text entry fields. There's plenty to choose from!

Chat/Calls

You can start chats and initiate calls from within Gmail itself. At the very bottom of the left menu, you'll see three icons—Hangouts, Chats, and Phone Calls. Click each one to view any contacts you may have that have these features enabled. You can start a Hangout (Google's Skype-like video calling service, covered in more depth later on in Part 3.8), text-based chat, or phone call by clicking a contact's name.

Tasks

Much like Microsoft Outlook, Gmail includes a Task list. You can add items to your task list, add new lists altogether, and set due dates. It's a very simple task manager, but like everything else in Gmail, it's accessible from any machine with an Internet browser.

YOUTUBE

We can't imagine the modern Internet without YouTube. YouTube is very tightly integrated with your Google account, so you're automatically signed in whenever you open the YouTube app.

Watching Videos

Perhaps the most obvious thing you'll want to do with the YouTube app is watch streaming videos online. This is easy and extremely addictive! You can search for videos using the YouTube search bar at the top of the YouTube app page, or you can browse around the featured videos underneath.

When you've found a video you'd like to watch, simply click it in the search results list. It'll start to play. Note that many popular YouTube videos and/or videos that use copyrighted material like songs may play an ad before the video starts. Try not to be too annoyed—this is how YouTube remains free and full of hilarious parodies, remixes, and reinterpretations that make it so much fun!

There are media controls in the lower left corner of the YouTube player window where you can pause the video, control the volume, and see the elapsed and remaining time. In the lower right corner, you'll find some additional features, including (from left to right) Watch Later, Settings (where you can adjust the speed and quality of the video playback depending on your system and connection speed), Theatre Mode and Full Screen. Theatre Mode is sort of halfway between the normal YouTube display and Full Screen—try it out to see if it's for you. Full Screen, of course, is the best way to get your computer to mimic a television.

To the right of the video player, you'll see a list of related videos. This is great if you're entertaining yourself with one of the millions of YouTube memes out there (literal music videos, inappropriate music for movies, and Sharky the Pit Bull are some of our classic favorites).

You can thumbs up or thumbs down a video, or comment on it to take advantage of YouTube's social features. Scroll down to see the comments underneath the player. We're not going to lie to you here. YouTube comments can be…rough. We ask in the name of a brighter Internet future that if you're going to participate in YouTube commentary that you 1) don't feed the trolls, and 2) don't be a troll! Trolls, for the record, are Internet users who say inflammatory and frequently extremely offensive things for the purpose of eliciting a reaction, and you're probably going to come across them if you spend much time on the site.

Account Features

There's more to YouTube than simply browsing around and watching online videos. Using your Google account, you can create playlists of YouTube videos, subscribe to other users' channels, access a list of your recently viewed videos, and create a Watch Later list for when you just don't have time for that twenty minute documentary on urban beekeeping but are really interested. You'll find all of these options in the YouTube menu to the left of the main content area. You can click the menu button next to the YouTube logo in the top left corner to hide and reveal these extra features as needed.

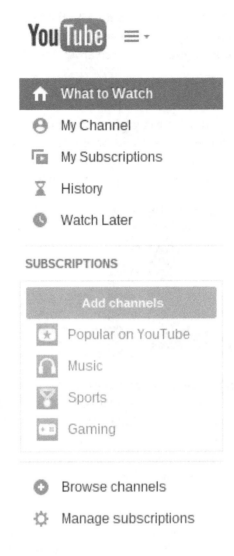

To subscribe to a YouTube channel, locate the channel's owner on a video page, or, if you know the owner's name, just search for it using the YouTube search bar. Then, on their profile page, click the red Subscribe button. You'll then find new content from that user under Subscriptions in the YouTube menu.

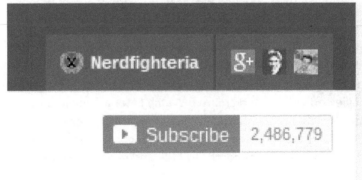

To create a playlist of YouTube videos, click Add to underneath the creators' names on the video's page. Before you can take advantage of this, though, you'll need to set up your Google+ profile and your YouTube channel page. The first time you click Add to you'll be prompted to set all of this up if you haven't already.

Who I Was in High School

vlogbrothers ☑

▶ Subscribe   2,486,779

╋ Add to   ◀ Share   ••• More

Uploading Videos
If you'd like to upload your own videos to YouTube, just click the Upload button in the top right corner.

You'll need to set up your Google+ profile and your YouTube channel page before you can upload, but after that you can easily upload and share your videos. Videos can be private or only shared with certain people. You can also choose to enable or disable public comments, depending on your preference.

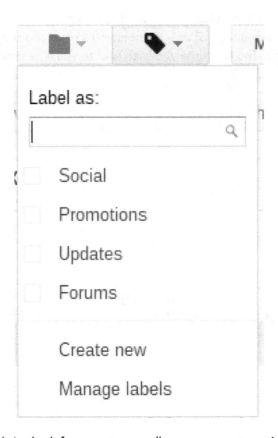

You can click on your labels in the left menu to see all messages categorized with them. You can also search for labels in the Gmail search bar.

CALCULATOR

The Calculator app is a simple utility and a rare example of an app that doesn't open inside a Chrome window. It performs basic calculations—no more, no less. It's nice to have a calculator that appears outside of all your other Chrome tabs and windows, though, and you may want to consider pinning it to your Chromebook's shelf if you find yourself using it time and time again.

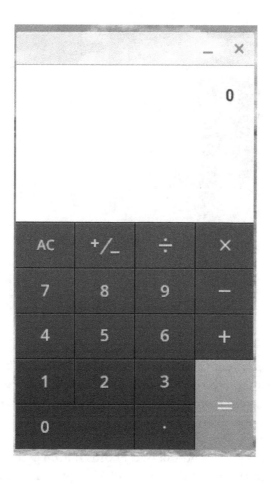

CAMERA

Most Chromebook devices include at least a forward-facing camera, and the camera app is your go-to for Chromebook or Slate selfie purposes. The Camera app includes several filters to add fun (and sometimes funny) effects to your photos, a timer, and mirroring, which reverses an image so that it would match what you see in the mirror. It's a simple single-action app, but it's great to have when you need a quick snap for a profile pic or message.

CHROME REMOTE DESKTOP

Chrome Remote Desktop (CRD) is similar in function to Windows Remote Desktop and Apple Remote Desktop. Basically, it allows you to view and control a different computer or device remotely. It's incredibly helpful for Instructional Technology (IT) professionals and for getting help with your system.

For Chrome Remote Desktop to work, both machines must be running the CRD app, which can be installed in Chrome in any operating system, as long as the Google Chrome browser is installed. To open a connection, the remote user needs to open the CRD app and click Share. This will generate an access code, which the remote user will give to you. Enter the access code into CRD on your Chromebook, and you'll be able to see and control the remote machine.

GOOGLE+ PHOTOS

The Google+ Photos app is your Chromebook's photo manager. It's not entirely unlike Apple's iPhoto, but it is very tightly integrated with Google+, for better or worse. Google+ Photos helps you consolidate your photos, organize them and share them through Google+.

To get started, open the app using the Apps button. You'll need to sign up for Google+ if you haven't already done so. From there, you can import photos from your Google+ account, your Chromebook, or Google Drive by clicking the Add Photos button in the top right corner. You can then organize your photos into albums, share them through Google+, delete them, or save them to your Chromebook or your Google Drive account.

The Photos app includes the ability to rotate the photo and/or enhance it using the Enhance tool, which appears when you move your mouse over the photo. This is an automatic fix rather than a set of manual features. For serious photo editing, we recommend Pixlr Editor or another photo app from the Web Store.

GOOGLE KEEP

Google Keep is a note-taking app that aims to compete with products like Microsoft OneNote or Evernote. You can add notes and reminders lists that will sync with the online version of Keep at keep.google.com. There's also an Android app that you can download for your smartphone or tablet.

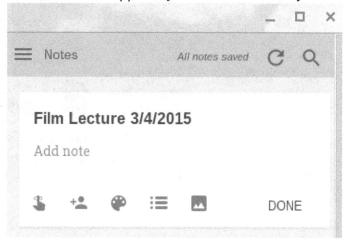

Notes in Keep can include lists and images, and you can share them with others. It's a handy way to keep yourself organized, and it's a quick note-taking app for those times when you don't need all the bells and whistles of Google Docs.

GOOGLE MAPS AND GOOGLE MY MAPS

Google Maps is, in our opinion, the best free online maps service in the game, and it's built right into your Chromebook.

To use Google Maps, type the address, town or place name (The House on the Rock, Yellowstone National Park, etc.), into the search box in the top left corner. From there, you can get directions to that address by clicking Directions, or you can save the location for later reference. In the example above, you can see that Google Maps also pulled reviews and contact information for us, since we searched for a popular tourist destination.

In the bottom left corner, you will see a box labeled Earth. Clicking this box will toggle Google Earth—a beautiful satellite mode that will give you a photographic aerial view of your mapped area. You can switch back to Map mode by clicking the Map square in the bottom left corner.

In the bottom right corner of the screen, you'll find a few controls for adjusting your Google Maps experience. The Target button is a shortcut to your current location. Click it to get a map of your immediate surroundings. Beneath it, the + and - buttons let you zoom in and out. You can zoom out to a planetary view if you like!

The little yellow man in the controls area is the Google Streetview operator. Drag him from this menu to a spot on the map to enter Streetview. Streetview is a great way to check out a neighborhood or to explore the world a little. The screenshot below is the view from beneath the Eiffel Tower.

Google My Maps

The Google My Maps app is somewhat confusingly named, but it's extremely useful if you ever need to share directions with a large group of people. It's basically Google Maps, but slightly remixed in such a way that users can save maps in Google Drive and import layers of data into the Maps interface. For example, you might have a spreadsheet listing addresses that you'd like to add. You can also add placemarks and give them your own description or draw lines or add Google Maps routes and directions. Once your custom map is complete, you can share it using a generated link that can be copied and pasted wherever you need it, or through email, Google+, Facebook, and Twitter. This is a very handy feature for invitations or websites.

GOOGLE FORMS

Google Forms is a form generator that works closely with Google Sheets. If you've ever used Survey Monkey before, you should feel right at home in Forms. Your Forms questions can include multiple choice, text, checkboxes, scales, grids, dates and times, and you can make as many answers required as you like. Once your form is complete, you can invite people to fill it out through a URL or through email invitations. Responses will be automatically recorded in a Google Sheets spreadsheet for analysis (though you can turn this off if you'd prefer to keep all responses inside the Forms app for some reason).

Page 1 of 1

Board Meeting in March

Form Description

Question Title	Which of the following dates can you attend a board meeting?
Help Text	Choose as many dates as you like.
Question Type	Multiple choice ▾ ☐ Go to page based on answer

March 7
March 21
March 28

or Add "Other"

▸ Advanced settings

Done   ✓ Required question

GOOGLE DRAWINGS

The Google Drawings app allows you to create and annotate images. You can also insert text boxes, shapes, and lines. The freeform drawing tool is called Scribbles, and you'll find it under Insert > Line. Drawings shouldn't be compared to giants like Photoshop or Illustrator. Its closest relative is probably Microsoft Paint. Of course, any images you create in Drawings are saved in Drive, meaning it's very easy to insert them into other Drive apps, like Google Slides or Google Docs.

PLAY MUSIC, PLAY BOOKS, AND PLAY MOVIES

These three media apps make it possible to enjoy music, books, and movies purchased from the Google Play Store and from elsewhere on your Chromebook.

Play Music

The Play Music app includes an optional subscription that gives you access to millions of streaming songs without any ads. First time users generally get some sort of free trial offer, but after that it costs $9.99 a month.

If you decide to use the Standard version of Play Music, you'll then be given the option to upload your music from other sources, including iTunes. To do this, you may need to navigate to Google Play Music from the device that has your tunes on it, which is probably not your relatively low-memory Chromebook. However, once you've uploaded your library (from anywhere), you can enjoy it streaming through Play Music on your Chromebook and on most other devices by installing the Play Music app. You can upload up to 50,000 songs free of charge.

Play Books

Play Books is an ebook app that's half bookshelf and half bookstore. At the top of the Play Books app, you'll see two links—My Books and Shop Books. Any books you've purchased through the Shop link (or through the Google Play Store on a different computer) will appear under My Books. Buying books is identical to buying apps or extensions. If you don't already have a credit card number on file with Google, you'll be prompted to enter one. Of course, there are a number of classics and other free titles in the Play Store, so there's no need to whip out the plastic if you don't want to!

Any books you buy through Play Books will be available on your Android smartphone or tablet as well, and the Play Books app will keep everything synced up. This means that no matter what device you're using to read, your current read will open to exactly where you left off.

Play Movies

The Play Movies app allows you to enjoy movies and television shows purchased through the Google Play Store. Just like the Play Books app, Play Movies includes a Shop link where you can find streaming video to watch.

Google Play movies and television shows can be bought (you can stream them as many times as you like) or rented (you can only stream them during a certain amount of time). There are often pretty good deals on the Play Store—for example, at the time of writing, Star Trek was on offer in HD for just $4.99.

GOOGLE CALENDAR

Google Calendar is a great calendar tool, particularly since it's so widely used and importable into a variety of other calendaring systems. It's easy to use, available through google.com/calendar on any computer with a web browser, and will notify you of upcoming events so you never miss a thing.

Adding a New Calendar Event

To add a new event to Google Calendar, click the red Create button in the top left corner.

Enter as much or as little information about your event as you need. Keep in mind that Google Calendar has some powerful time management features to help keep you on track. It will send notifications before your event, at an interval of your choosing. You can also set recurring events by clicking the "Repeat" checkbox.

Adding and Sharing Calendars

The Google Calendar system includes the ability to set up multiple calendars. Maybe you'd like to have one personal calendar and then a shared family calendar or a team project calendar. To add a new calendar, click the boxed downward pointing arrow to the right of the My Calendars heading in the left menu. This will take you to the New Calendar setup screen. At the bottom, you'll see options for controlling your calendar's privacy and inviting people to view and/or add to the calendar.

Hiding Calendars

We've found that it's very easy to get enthusiastic about calendars, only to find yourself drowning in calendar entries. Fortunately, it's easy to temporarily hide calendars to help clean up your view. To hide a calendar, just click the little colored square next to its name in the My Calendars list. This won't delete anything, but it will hide all events associated with that calendar so you can focus on the events that need your attention.

[6]

MAKING IT YOUR OWN WITH CUSTOMIZATIONS

This chapter will cover:
- Changing the Appearance
- Device
- Searching
- People
- Date and Time
- Privacy
- Web Content
- Languages
- Downloads
- HTTPS/SSL Certificates
- Google Cloud Print
- Startup
- Accessibility
- Powerwash and Reset
- Supervised Accounts
- Troubleshooting
-

If you already have the watch, then you can skip right ahead to the next chapter. How's that for ridiculously simple?! This chapter is just for readers curious about all the different watches available.

The Apple Watch comes in several different.

In this section, we'll talk about several ways you can customize your Chromebook to suit your unique needs and personality. There are quite a few useful tweaks available for Chromebook, and we'll walk you through them all here. We'll also show you how to manage user accounts on your Chromebook, including children's accounts, and give you a few tips for troubleshooting and finding help.

To open your Chromebook settings, click the area of the screen that displays the time, wireless connection, battery, and your profile picture in the bottom right corner. Then click Settings. We're going to examine each heading that appears on this screen.

CHANGING THE APPEARANCE

The Appearance heading in Settings covers, well, the appearance of your Chromebook. Here you can set your desktop wallpaper to a custom image by clicking Set Wallpaper. This will open up a dialog box where you can browse your Chromebook for the image file you'd like to use. You can also click the Get Themes button to be taken to the Themes area of the Chrome Web Store. Themes add a graphic layer to your Chrome window—an image or color for new tab windows and colors and designs for the menu area. There are plenty of fun themes to choose from, and if you change your mind about any of them, you can always click Reset to Default Theme to go back to Chrome's original appearance.

Appearance

Set wallpaper...	Get themes	Reset to default theme

☑ Show Home button

gadchick.com/ Change

☐ Always show the bookmarks bar

You can also set a home page here if you like. First, click Show Home button to tell Chrome to show the Home button in your Chrome browser as a special shortcut to your home page. Click Change to add a new home page. This is the page that will be displayed every time you open Chrome.

Finally, you can choose to always show the bookmarks bar in Chrome here as well.

DEVICE

The Device heading is a pretty important Settings area, even if it's a little bit of a catchall. There are some really useful options and features tucked away here.

Device

Change settings specific to your device and peripherals.

Battery...	Stored data...

Touchpad speed: ———————————

Touchpad settings	Keyboard settings	Display settings

First, you can take a look at what's using your battery by clicking the Battery button. This is a great way to maximize your Chromebook's battery even further if you need to. Just close the apps that are sucking up the most juice.

The Stored Data button is also a fascinating glimpse into what Chrome is doing with every page and app you visit or use. Check out what our Chromebook has to say about weather.com.

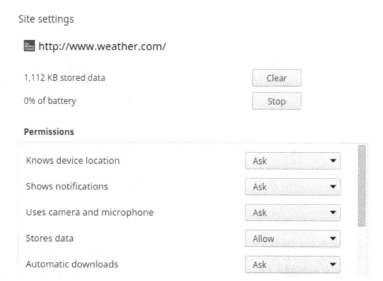

We can see how much stored data from this site is eating into our hard disc (in this case, not very much), as well as how much of the battery it's using. Right now, it's not running, so it requires 0% of our battery. Then we can see a fairly extensive list of permissions for the site, and change them as we see fit. For this example, we may want to allow this site to know our Chromebook's location so that it will always give us the weather of our current spot.

Underneath the battery and stored data information, you'll find some options for configuring your touchpad, keyboard, and display. You can adjust your touchpad's speed to match that of your fingers using the slider, and you can also change the direction the page moves when you scroll and enable or disable tap-to-click. By clicking Keyboard, you can view the shortcut display mentioned earlier in the book, and you can also change the behavior of certain keyboard keys if you like—namely Search, CTRL, and ALT.

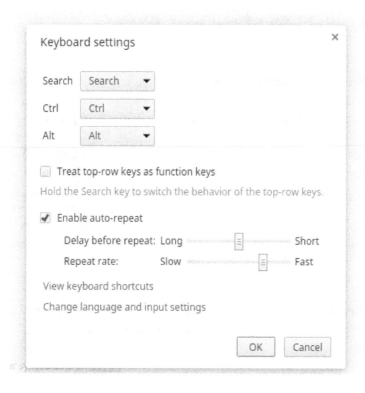

SEARCHING

One of our favorite things about Google products is their flexibility. It would stand to reason that the proprietary Google OS based on Google's browser would limit users to the Google search engine for the Chrome omnibox, but that's not the case. In the Search heading, you can change Chrome's search engine to Yahoo!, Bing, Ask, or AOL.

Search

Set which search engine is used when searching from the omnibox.

Google ▼   Manage search engines...

The Manage Search Engines button finds additional search engines, like YouTube search, for example. You can add these highly specific searches as your omnibox default if you'd like (though for most users we do recommend sticking with a general internet-wide search engine).

PEOPLE

Under the People heading, you can accomplish two important tasks. First, you can manage what aspects of your Chromebook sync with your Google Account by clicking Advanced Sync Settings. By default, everything is selected, but you can adjust as needed. You can also choose how you'd like Google Chrome to encrypt your data.

The other feature under People is the ability to manage logins on your Chromebook. More than one Google user can sign in, and you can manage other users as needed. You can decide whether or not to enable a Guest account and supervised users (which we'll talk about in more detail shortly) and whether or not to restrict sign-in to certain users. You can also add users to your Chromebook here.

At this point, you'll need to click Show Advanced Settings to see the rest of the Chrome settings menu!

DATE AND TIME

There's not much here besides the ability to change your time zone and switch your system clock to 24-hour time. Chrome will set the date and time automatically based on your time zone.

Date and time

Time zone: (UTC-6:00) Central Standard Time (Chicago)   ▾

☐ Use 24-hour clock

Date and time are set automatically.

PRIVACY

Your privacy settings give you some control over how much information your Chromebook shares with the rest of the world. Google uses quite a few prediction services in order to load pages fast and get you where you want to go, but you may not want all of them accessing your personal information, search engine terms, etc. To disable any of these services, deselect them under the Privacy heading.

The Content settings button includes several Chrome options, like pop-up blocking, location tracking, JavaScript settings, automatic downloads and more. Most of these settings include a Manage exceptions button. As you surf the web, Chrome will ask you if you'd like to make these exceptions. For example, when Chrome blocks a pop-up, it will notify you of the action and then ask if you'd like to allow pop-ups once or always for that site. You can then revoke those exceptions later if you need to in Content Settings.

Generally we recommend leaving these settings with their defaults, as we think there's a good balance between end-user protection and convenience of use. Nevertheless, you may occasionally need to turn off the pop-up blocker or adjust another one of these settings, and it's good to know where to find them.

WEB CONTENT

The web content settings allow you to change the default font size and page zoom for web pages. You can also choose what sort of font you'd like Chrome to display as a default.

LANGUAGES

The Languages heading allows you to turn automatic translation offers on and off. You can also manage the languages you'd like to use with Chromebook by clicking the Language and input settings button. You can add more than one by clicking the Add button in the lower left corner. The language at the top of your list will be your default language, but adding additional languages gives you the ability to set up keyboard input options so that you can quickly switch languages as needed.

DOWNLOADS

Here you can change the way your Chromebook handles downloads. Perhaps the most useful feature here is the ability to change the default downloads location to something more accessible than the Downloads folder. Or, if you prefer, you can tell Chrome that you want it to always ask you where you want to save downloads. You can disable Google Drive here as well, though we don't recommend it.

HTTPS/SSL CERTIFICATES

This area of your settings allows you to view and manage security certificates stored on your computer. The average user won't have too many reasons to make changes here, but it's good to know it's there if you're ever prompted to install or uninstall a certificate.

GOOGLE CLOUD PRINT

Google Cloud Print is Google's printing service. It allows users to send a print job over the web to their printer, rather than the traditional methods of wired or wireless printer connections. To use it, you'll need to connect your printer to your Google Cloud Print account. You'll find instructions and more information about this by clicking Learn more under the Google Cloud Print heading.

STARTUP

The On Startup heading tells Chrome what to do the first time you open it. You can start with a new tab page, or open the pages that you had open during your last use (the default option). You can also set a page or group of pages that you'd like to open. This is a great way to open your email, Facebook, the news, and your favorite blog without having to do anything but start Google Chrome.

On startup

○ Open the New Tab page

◉ Continue where you left off

○ Open a specific page or set of pages. Set pages

ACCESSIBILITY

The accessibility heading provides a suite of features designed to make Chromebook more accessible for individuals with impaired vision or certain motor disabilities. Select as many as you like to make your Chromebook experience more comfortable for you.

There is an additional collection of accessibility apps and extensions in the Web Store as well. To view them, click Add additional accessibility features.

POWERWASH AND RESET

The powerwash and reset options are located at the very bottom of the advanced settings screen. Powerwash is the panic button. This extreme step will completely erase everything on your Chromebook and restore it to factory settings. It can be used as an absolutely last-ditch troubleshooting measure, but just remember that it's permanent—there's no recovering from a Powerwash (though of course you can re-download anything you've purchased through Google, and since almost everything on Chromebook is a web app, you won't lose any of your files stored in Google Drive). Powerwash is also the thing to do if you're selling or giving away your Chromebook.

A less drastic approach is the Reset button. This doesn't wipe your device, but it does restore all system settings to their original defaults. If you've played with your configuration and decided you prefer the original, just hit Reset to get back to square one without losing your apps or data.

SUPERVISED ACCOUNTS

If you have any children in your house, you may want to set up supervised accounts for them. This will allow them to use your Chromebook, but with a few restrictions designed to keep them safe and you sane. You can restrict web pages and content for supervised users, and you can log in anytime to chrome.com/manage to monitor the account.

To add a supervised user, click Add user on the sign-in screen. A sign-in box will appear. Click Create a supervised user (in blue) on the right side of the box to get started.

Next, you'll name the account and set a password and profile picture. Supervised users aren't Google Accounts users, so there's no need to set up a unique username. You can also set a password that's easy to remember, since it's for a local account instead of an online one.

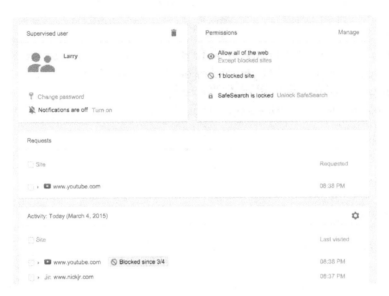

At chrome.com/manage, you can change the supervised user's password, set restricted sites, and deal with requests to unblock sites from the user, as seen above.

TROUBLESHOOTING AND MAINTAINING YOUR CHROMEBOOK

One of the best things about Chromebook is its simplicity—unlike more complex operating system software like Windows or Mac OSX, there's really very little that can go wrong. However, things can and do happen sometimes, and we'll walk you through some quick and easy troubleshooting methods here.

Check Your Battery

Also known as the "is it plugged in?" step, this is a frequent culprit in Chromebook problems. Check to be sure that your charger is connected and plugged in before you jump to any conclusions as to why your Chromebook won't wake up.

Restart

When in doubt, reboot. This often is all it takes to fix frozen systems or other irritating problems. Thanks to most Chrome apps' constant background saving processes, you rarely need to worry about losing work when you do this.

If you're having problems with an app, you can always try closing it and reopening it. If that doesn't work, you may want to try removing it from your device and then re-downloading it from the Web Store.

Getting Help and Contacting Support

If you're stuck with a Chromebook problem, try the Get Help app. It's a searchable tour of your Chromebook's features and may provide the answer you need. If that doesn't work, you might try the Google user forums at https://support.google.com chromebook-central. Here you'll find frequently asked questions, user forums where you can search for other people with your issue (or post it yourself), and more. You'll find power Google users to be a pretty informed bunch, and the forums are an excellent resource when you run into trouble.

To get official support for your Chromebook, you can either request a call or start a chat session with a Google technician. To do this, visit support.google.com/Chromebook and click Contact Us in the top right corner.

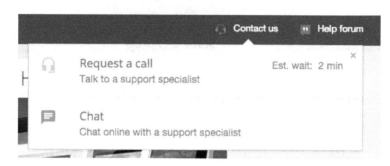

Updating Your Chromebook

Chromebook keeps itself up-to-date for the most part, so the only thing you need to do is be sure that it's regularly online and in use. Chrome will take care of the rest! If you ever need to see what version of Chrome you're running, you can do so by visiting Chrome Settings. Then click About Chrome OS at the top. This will display your device's update status, as well as its current version.

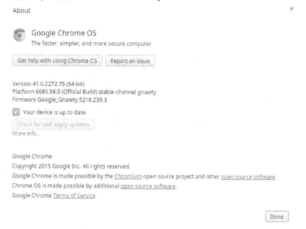

It's a good idea to periodically check that your system is updating itself. You may occasionally need to click Check for and apply updates to manually perform an update check. Sometimes new updates require a system restart, fortunately, most Chromebooks restart within seconds!

APPENDIX A: SPECS

Specification	Pixelbook	Surface Laptop	MacBook
Software	Chrome OS	Windows 10 S	macOS High Sierra
Display	12.3 inches	13.5 inches	12 inches
Resolution	2400 x 1600	2256 x 1504	2304 x 1440
Processor (base)	Intel Core i5 (seventh-gen)	Intel Core i5 (seventh-gen)	Intel Core m3 (1.2GHz, dual-core, seventh-gen)
Processor (max)	Intel Core i7 (seventh-gen)	Intel Core i7 (seventh-gen)	Intel Core i7 (1.4GHz, dual-core, seventh-gen)
RAM (base)	8GB	4GB	8GB
RAM(max)	16GB	16GB	16GB
Ports	USB-C, 3.5mm headphone jack	USB 3.0, 3.5mm headphone jack, Mini DisplayPort	USB-C, 3.5mm headphone jack
Storage	128GB, 256GB, 512GB	128GB, 256GB, 512GB, 1TB	256GB, 512GB
Weight	2.4 pounds	2.76 pounds	2.03 pounds
Starting price	$999	$999	$1,299

APPENDIX B: SHORTCUT KEYS

Popular shortcuts

- Open the Google Assistant: Press

- Search your device, apps, web and more: Press

- Open the status area (where your account picture appears): Press

- Take a screenshot: Press Ctrl +

- Take a partial screenshot: Press Ctrl + Shift +   , then click and drag

- Turn Caps Lock on or off: Press Alt + Search

- Lock your screen: Press Search + L

- Sign out of your Google Account: Press Ctrl + Shift + q (twice)

-

All other shortcuts

Note: If you're using a Windows or Mac keyboard, use the Windows key or Command key in place of the Search key.

Tabs and windows	
Open a new window	Ctrl + n
Open a new window in incognito mode	Ctrl + Shift + n

Open a new tab	Ctrl + t
Open a file in the browser	Ctrl + o
Close the current tab	Ctrl + w
Close the current window	Ctrl + Shift + w
Reopen the last tab or window you closed	Ctrl + Shift + t
Go to tabs 1-8 in the window	Ctrl + 1 through Ctrl + 8
Go to the last tab in the window	Ctrl + 9
Go to the next tab in the window	Ctrl + Tab
Go to the previous tab in the window	Ctrl + Shift + Tab
Switch quickly between windows	Press & hold Alt, tap Tab until you get to the window you want to open, then release.
Open the window you used least recently	Press & hold Alt + Shift, tap Tab until you get to the window you want to open, then release.
Go to previous page in your browsing history	Alt + left arrow
Go to the next page in your browsing history	Alt + right arrow
Open the link in a new tab in the background	Press Ctrl and click a link

Open the link in a new tab and switch to the new tab	Press Ctrl + Shift and click a link
Open the link in a new window	Press Shift and click a link
Open the link in the tab	Drag the link to the tab's address bar
Open the link in a new tab	Drag the link to a blank area on the tab strip
Open the webpage in a new tab	Type a web address (URL) in the address bar, then press Alt + Enter
Return the tab to its original position	While dragging the tab, press Esc
Dock a window on the left	Alt + [
Dock a window on the right	Alt +]

Page & Web Browser

Page up	Alt or Search and up arrow
Page down	Alt or Search and down arrow
Scroll down the web page	Space bar
Go to top of page	Ctrl + Alt and up arrow
Go to bottom of page	Ctrl + Alt and down arrow
Print your current page	Ctrl + p
Save your current page	Ctrl + s

Reload your current page	Ctrl + r
Reload your current page without using cached content	Ctrl + Shift + r
Zoom in on the page	Ctrl and +
Zoom out on the page	Ctrl and -
Reset zoom level	Ctrl + 0
Stop the loading of your current page	Esc
Right-click a link	Press Alt and click a link
Open the link in a new tab in the background	Press Ctrl and click a link
Save the link as a bookmark	Drag link to bookmarks bar
Save your current webpage as a bookmark	Ctrl + d
Save all open pages in your current window as bookmarks in a new folder	Ctrl + Shift + d
Search the current page	Ctrl + f
Go to the next match for your search	Ctrl + g or Enter
Go to the previous match for your search	Ctrl + Shift + g or Shift + Enter
Perform a Google search	[*] or Ctrl + k or Ctrl + e

Add www. and .com to your input in the address bar, then open the page	Ctrl + Enter
View page source	Ctrl + u
Show or hide the Developer Tools panel	Ctrl + Shift + i
Show or hide the DOM Inspector	Ctrl + Shift + j
Show or hide the bookmarks bar	Ctrl + Shift + b
Open the History page	Ctrl + h
Open the Downloads page	Ctrl + j

System & Display Settings

Open the Files app	Alt + Shift + m
Preview a file in the Files app	Select the file, then press Space
Display hidden files in the Files app	Ctrl + .
Open the status area (where your account picture appears)	☰ or Shift + Alt + s
Click icons 1-8 on your shelf	Alt + 1 through Alt + 8
Click the last icon on your shelf	Alt + 9
Use F keys (F1 to F12)	Search + 1 through Search + =
See your notifications	Alt + Shift + n

Change screen resolution	Ctrl + Shift and + or -
Reset screen resolution to default	Ctrl + Shift + 0
Rotate screen 90 degrees	Ctrl + Shift + [↻]
Switch to the next user	Ctrl + Alt + .
Switch to the previous user	Ctrl + Alt + ,

Text Editing

Turn Caps Lock on or off	Alt + Search
Select everything on the page	Ctrl + a
Select the content in the address bar	Ctrl + L or Alt + d
Select the next word or letter	Ctrl + Shift and right arrow
Select text to the end of the line	Shift + Search and right arrow
Select text to the beginning of the line	Shift + Search and left arrow
Select previous word or letter	Ctrl + Shift and left arrow
Move to the end of the next word	Ctrl and right arrow
Move to the start of the previous word	Ctrl and left arrow

Go to end of document	Ctrl + Search and right arrow
Go to beginning of document	Ctrl + Search and left arrow
Copy selected content to the clipboard	Ctrl + c
Paste content from the clipboard	Ctrl + v
Paste content from the clipboard as plain text	Ctrl + Shift + v
Cut	Ctrl + x
Delete the previous word	Ctrl + Backspace
Delete the next letter (forward delete)	Alt + Backspace
Undo your last action	Ctrl + z
Redo your last action	Ctrl + Shift + z
Switch between the keyboard languages you've set. Learn how to choose your keyboard language.	Ctrl + Shift + Space
Switch to the previous keyboard language you were using. Learn how to choose your keyboard language.	Ctrl + Space
Dim keyboard (for backlit keyboards only)	Alt + [▢]
Make keyboard brighter (for backlit keyboards only)	Alt + [▢]

Accessibility

Learn how to make your Pixelbook accessible.

Turn ChromeVox (spoken feedback) on or off	Ctrl + Alt + z
Turn on high contrast mode	Ctrl + Search + h
Highlight the launcher button on your shelf	Shift + Alt + L
Highlight the next item on your shelf	Shift + Alt + L, then Tab or right arrow
Highlight the previous item on your shelf	Shift + Alt + L, then Shift + Tab or left arrow
Open the highlighted button on your shelf	Shift + Alt + L, then Space or Enter
Remove the highlight from a button on your shelf	Shift + Alt + L, then Esc
Switch focus between: • Status area (where your account picture appears) • Launcher • Address bar • Bookmarks bar (if visible) • The webpage that's open • Downloads bar (if visible)	Ctrl + [←]
Highlight the bookmarks bar (if shown)	Alt + Shift + b
Highlight the row with the address bar	Shift + Alt + t

| Open right-click menu for highlighted item | Shift + [*] |

GOOGLE APPS

INTRODUCTION

Chances are you grew up a Word and Office user. Maybe you were a rebel and committed your herd to OpenOffice, or, dare I say, WordPerfect—but for the majority of people, our lives were loyal to Microsoft.

In 2005, a small little startup named Upstartle developed something unheard of at the time: a web-based word processor called Writely. It pioneered the idea of writing on the "cloud" and changed the way people thought about word processing.

Google noticed the little upstart, and in 2006, they acquired the company. The software was abandoned and turned into what everyone knows today as Google Docs. It disrupted the industry—namely, Microsoft's industry.

Today, Google has a whole suite of productivity apps; from documents to spreadsheets, you can do just about anything from the cloud. Microsoft and Apple have each made big attempts to create cloud-based environments of their own for office productivity, but Google pioneered the idea and its collaborative, online environment make it hard to beat. It's become so feature-rich that many businesses are finding it to be the preferred way to conduct business.

If you are thinking about making the switch to Google, or have already made the switch but want to make sure you are using it correctly, then this guide will walk you through it. It will show you all the basic features to make sure you can get up and running as quick as possible.

Let's get started!

GOOGLE DRIVE

[1]

THE GOOGLE DRIVE CRASH COURSE

This chapter will cover:
* Why is it free?
* Creating files
* Finding files

Why Is It Free?

You are probably wondering "If it's so great then why is it free?" You don't give away great software for free, right? There has to be a catch! There's always a catch! Are they taking your data and selling it on the black market? First, no! Second, not everyone is out to get you, so just simmer down!

The Google you know gives all their tools away. How exactly do they make money? Does some rich guy donate a penny every time someone Googles "cute cat photos"? Definitely not—no one is that wealthy! Google makes money by selling ads, cloud services, selling apps, and a number of other things which all adds up to billions of dollars.

So there are ads in Google Docs? Nope! It all goes back to Google's business model. Unlike Microsoft, who is trying to make money off its software, Google is trying to make money off its service. It wants schools and businesses to use its enterprise services.

The Google Docs that we use is free; but for businesses that want to add dozens of workers, or schools who want to add hundreds of students, there is a charge.

If you are a small business, then there's a good chance you could probably make do with the free version. Plus, if Google is managing your company's email account, then you are paying for the service already.

Google Drive Overview

Every computer has "local" storage, which is where all the stuff (files, photos, documents), is stored directly on the computer. Windows computers have File/System Explorer, Mac Computers have Finder, and Google has Google Drive—it's the same concept you are accustomed to on your home computer, but it's all online.

Google Drive is basically an online version of a file directory; whatever you create in Google is stored here—think of it like Google's version of DropBox. In fact, you can also store files here—photos, videos, PDFs—whatever you want.

To get started, go to drive.google.com. If you are not signed in to a Google account, then you'll be greeted by a lovely screen that looks a little like the one below:

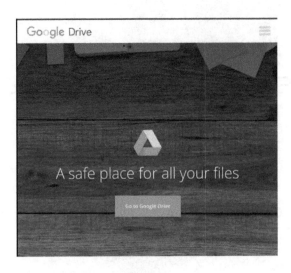

Click that "Go to Google Drive" blue button and you'll see an option that looks like the below:

While Google Docs is free to use, you do need a Google account to use it. So that's the catch, right? Free to use, but you have to pay to get a Google account? Nope! A Google account is also free. If you use Gmail, then you already have one, and can use that to sign in.

Once you are all signed in you'll see the main interface. The side pane is your main navigation. This is where you will see all of your folders. It's probably empty right now, unless you've started using it.

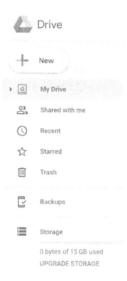

Two things to note here:
1. Shared with me—if people share documents or folders with you, they'll be here unless you move them.
2. Starred—to help you stay organized, you can "star" documents. When you "star" them, they will still be in your main directory, but they'll be here as well.

If you have the basic free plan, you'll have 15 GBs of storage. That's obviously a lot. Considering that a document is very small, you'll probably never want more—unless you are also using Google Drive to store videos and files, or to back up your entire computer.

Why on Earth would you want to pay to back up your computer on the cloud? Because it's surprising cheap! The rates below are what you can expect—they might go up after this book is printed, but not by much since they've been this low for a while.

Most people have around 200 GBs of data floating around. That means, for less than a dinner for two at Olive Garden, you can safely know that your data is protected online!

Why back it up online? Two reasons:
1. What if your house floods or burns down and you don't have time to get your computer. Think of all the memories you would lose that are stored on your computer.
2. What if you are away on business or a family trip and you really need a document. It's safely online and you can access it anytime.

If you want to back up your entire computer to Google Drive, you just need to download some software that will sync your computer to the cloud. That means if you save a new file, that file automatically goes to the cloud and you don't have to do a thing. You can also pick and choose what folders are synced to the cloud. To get the software, go to the address below:
https://support.google.com/drive/answer/2424368?co=GENIE.Platform%3DDesktDD&hl=en

Creating Files and Docs

Once you're ready to create either a document (such as a doc, spreadsheet or presentation), click the new button in the left menu pane:

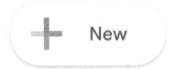

This will bring up several choices. The main three apps are on the bottom of this menu, but if you click "more" you can see some of the useful, but lesser used, Google Apps (I'm looking at you Google Jamboard!). You can also access this menu by right- clicking inside Google Drive:

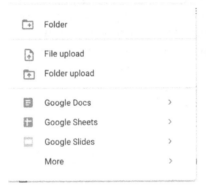

This is also where you'll go to upload files from your computer, or to create a new folder.

Creating folders will help you stay organized. You may, for example, have a recipe folder, or school folder, or a bills folder—you can have as many folders as you want. You can also create folders inside folders (and folders inside the folder you just created inside the folder—go ahead and figure that sentence out…I'll wait!). It's just like file organization on your computer.

If you want to create a folder within a folder, you can either open that folder up and select the new button, or you can right-click inside that open folder and select "Folder."

Starring and Sharing Files

Once the docs are created, you'll be able to right-click them at any time to bring up a new menu that's just for that specific file. You can add a star to it, rename it, preview it, and, of course, share it.

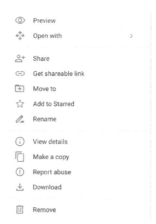

Once you click "Get sharable link" (the option for sharing a file with other people), you'll see something a little like this:

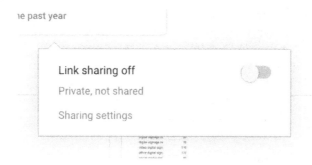

If it's white, like the above, it will note that sharing is off. To turn it on, just click that white box, and it will turn green and note that sharing is turned on. It will also give you a link to the document.

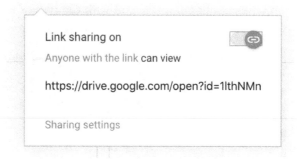

When it's on, by default, it's a non-public link. That means the only way someone is going to find it is if you give them the link.

If you click "Sharing settings" you'll get a few more options. You can email a person the link and also make them an editor, or give them all access.

Click the "Anyone with the link can view" drop down and you can manage the access, for example, if you only want certain people that you email to see it—note: if you select this option, they will need to be signed into a Google Account (the one you used in the email name in the box under this), to see the doc.

If you select "More" you'll have a few more options. One is to make the file public. This means it's going to be searchable to anyone on Google and people may find it randomly—people you don't know—so it's best if you don't make your Google Sheet with the names and phone numbers of "People with excessive gas" public.

Find Files

Files are pretty easy to find when you are first getting started. But they add up quickly—especially if you are using them for school or business, or if you are backing up all the files on your computer.

Fortunately, Google has a search bar that works remarkably well—it's right on top of Google Drive. You don't have to know the name of the file—you can search for what's in the document. So if you can't remember what you named your Google Doc, but you know it had the line "And that is why I love competitive dog grooming" (yes, it's a thing!), then just type in that phrase and it will find your doc.

If it's returning too many results—because you have obviously written countless scholarly papers on the subject of competitive dog grooming—then click that little arrow next to the search bar.

That brings up an advanced search. You'll be able to search by owner, by those that are starred, when it was lasted opened, what kind of file it is, and more. Once you've added in all your filters, just hit search, and it will return results in seconds.

GOOGLE DOCS

[1]

GOOGLE DOCS CRASH COURSE

This chapter will cover:
- Why use Word?
- The Crash Course
- Getting Started

Should I Throw Away Word and Never Look Back?

Before getting started, let's talk about the elephant in the room: Microsoft Word!

Does Google Docs make Word irrelevant? It really depends on the user. For most people, Google Docs can probably accomplish what you want to do.

Microsoft is paid software, but it's also a lot more powerful. If you are running macros, or doing mail mergers, and need other advanced features, then you'll probably want to stick with Word. There are add-ons for Google Docs, but they just don't beat what you'll find in the full version of Microsoft Word.

If you are just doing basic writing, then Google Docs will be just fine. When it comes to collaboration, it's more than just fine; while Microsoft has made great strides towards making it easier to share and collaborate in Word, Google is the one who mastered the idea. Google also has plug-ins for editing tools such as Grammarly, and is making a big push to be more responsive to catching basic grammatical errors.

Personally, I use Google Docs almost daily, but I still have a copy of Word on my desktop, and that's what I use for my final draft. Once collaboration is finished, I copy and paste it into Word and apply all the final touches.

The Crash Course

Before we jump into creating our first document, I'll go over the main Google Docs toolbar. If you've ever used Word, then you'll probably know what most of these do already. If you ever get stuck, then hover over the icon and it will give you a description of what it does.

The first two icons are your undo, redo icons. This undoes or redoes whatever you just typed:

Next is the Print, spellcheck, and formatter. You probably know what the first two are. The last one is a handy little tool; it copies the format of the text. So let's say I have text that is bold, 14- point in size. I can highlight that text, select the paint roller, then click on the text I want to apply the style to. Instantly that text is changed to the same style.

The 100% is the zoom. If you want to zoom out to see more (but smaller) text on the screen, then click on that:

100% ▾

Fonts and style is next to that. This is where you can select the style (if it's a Heading, for example), the font family, the font size, and if you want to bold, italicize, underline, or change the color of the text.

The insert options is the next section. These are all the things you may want to insert into a doc. That includes a link, a comment, and an image:

Justification is next to that. If you want to right align, center align, or change the line spacing, you'll use these options:

If you want to create a numbered or bulleted list, you can use the next two icons; next to those are the indentation:

If you have formatting you want to reset, you can use the icon below. This is good if you've copied text from the web and you want to reset it to the default Google Docs text size:

The last two options change how you are viewing a document and to hide the toolbar:

That's a high-level overview. These things will make more sense as we go.

Getting Started

Okay, so how exactly do you use Google Docs? There are several ways, but the quickest is to just type in drive.google.com.

Once you have your Google account, then you are all set. Repeat the step above and the browser Window should look more like the below:

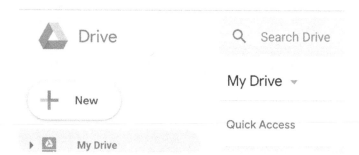

Docs really shines through its connection to Google Drive. Anything you start in Google Docs is automatically saved in your Google Drive account—no need to worry about losing work through power failures, device catastrophes, or really just about any other scenario. Changes are saved as you go, and so are the various versions of your document, so it's easy to revert to an earlier stage of a draft if you need to.

[3]

YOUR FIRST DOCUMENT

This chapter will cover:
- Creating your first document
- Titling your Google Doc
- Opening saved docs

Creating Your First Doc

Now that you have your account, let's create a document. Click on the "New" button and then hover over Google Docs; there are two options: Black document and From a template. For now, select "From a template." I'll cover templates a little bit later.

This is going to open up a new tab, and your Google Docs editor will appear.

If you're a Word or Pages user, then you'll be relieved to know everything is designed to work the same way. Many of the buttons look identical.

So, you don't need this book, right?! There's still a difference, and that's what we'll spend the most time with in this book.

Let's have some fun. Pretend the American Revolution is taking place in the year 2019 instead of the year 1776. The British have put fines on our beloved Internet usage, and the people have had enough! Why should you have to pay to see videos of adorable puppies on skateboards?

Michelle Obama is the leader of the American colonies. She's been working on the first draft of a proclamation with her first man, Barack Obama.

The first thing she needs is a title.

How to title your Google Doc

Look up in the upper left-hand corner of your Google Docs editor. See the text field that says, "Untitled Document." That's every Google Docs default title. Click on it.

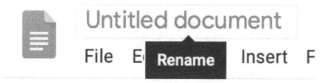

You can now add any title you want by typing. I'll pick something highly original: "The Declaration of Independence," but you can pick anything you want. When you finish, hit the enter key.

In a flash, watch that top bar change with your new title. As long as it shows the new title, then it worked.

Need even more assurance? Look to the right of it: it should say "All changes saved"? Guess what?! It saved!

All changes saved in Drive

It may not seem all that revolutionary today, but everything saves automatically. You don't need to hit CTRL S every few seconds. Google saves as you type. If you are the paranoid type, then you still can save manually.

Let's start things off by creating a headline for our doc. Let's go crazy and use Corsiva, 18-point font. You only live once, right?

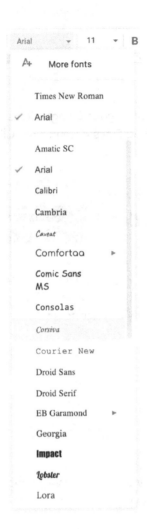

This hopefully feels familiar to you—it's essentially the same way you do it in other document editors. I bet you've used this type of toolbar hundreds of times before. Here's the take away here: icons that look like they do in another app tend to do the exact same thing they did in that other app.

My Glorious Heading!

So let's write the title and first paragraph of our declaration, then in a moment we'll send it off for review.

Everything is looking good so far, right? But what happens if there's a power outage? In a blink of a second, it all goes dark. How do we get back to where we left off?

Opening a saved document

Close your browser. Make sure Google Docs has completely gone away.

Now go right back to drive.google.com.

Unless you are on a public computer (like at a library), Google will show you all the files you have created. Since it was the last thing you worked on, you should see The Declaration of Independence right at the top in the Quick Access list.

If you are just getting started, it will also be the only doc you see, and you can access it below the quick access; it will look a "little" like this:

I say "little" because you might be in list view or you might be in grid view. What's the difference? List view looks like the above—it gives the name, who the owner is, and the time it was edited. Grid view is more of a thumbnail preview of the doc, like this:

Notice how author and time lasted edited is gone?

What's better? It's a preference, but if you are working with dozens of documents, then Grid view probably will not be ideal unless you need to see previews.

To toggle between the two, click these icons in the upper corner:

List is the horizontal lines, and grid is the six square boxes.

The top spot goes to documents that have been recently edited.

When you double-click on "The Declaration of Independence," it opens up in a new tab. It's basically the same as opening a document back up in Word—the difference: It's in the cloud.

You can also right-click it to see more options—one of them is "Open with" and you can open it by clicking Google Docs.

This option would be useful if you have a Chromebook that has other editing tools installed and you don't want to use Google Docs to edit it. For it to work, however, you need to have those other apps installed.

You can do that by going to the Chrome extensions store:

https://chrome.google.com/webstore/category/extensions

This is a marketplace for all things Chrome, and most of the extensions (or apps) are free. Just make sure you are using Chrome—hence the name. If you aren't, you can still see the page, but you'll be greeted with this subtle notice:

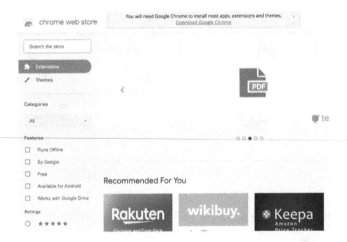

Like most Word Processing editors today, if you open it on a different device (i.e. smartphone or tablet), it's going to look pretty similar. Anything you change on those devices will reflect the document everywhere. It's all in the cloud.

Users of mobile devices (such as iPhones and iPads) can see Google Docs will need a native app to make edits, but what I'm talking about in this book is essentially identical on the apps.

Unfortunately, you'll need a separate app for every app you are using. So you need to get the Google Drive app and the Google Docs app—and if you plan on using Google Slides or Sheets, you'll need to get those apps too. Fortunately, they're free.

Your device has an app store, and that's where you'll download them—just type in the name of the app. The exception here is Fire tablets; these tablets have a not-so-nice relationship with Google that I won't go into here. Google won't put their apps in the app store because of that not-so-nice relationship. You can still install them, but you would need to do something called "side load app." That basically means you are downloading the app onto an SD card, putting the card into the tablet, and installing it manually. I'm not covering how to do that in this book, but if installing it on a Fire device is a must, then there are plenty of tutorials for that. Do so at your own risk, as it's not exactly supported by the device.

[4]

SHARING IS CARING

This chapter will cover:
- How to share docs
- Editing and collaborating

How To Share Your Google Docs

Google Docs is hands-down one of the easiest ways to work on a group document.

When two or more people are editing a document at the same time, you'll be able to see that person's cursor position and watch edits in real time. If you're concerned about losing work, remember that Google Docs saves the version history for you, so it's easy to revert if you need to. Click File > See revision history (or press CTRL+ALT+SHIFT+G). By default, revisions are shown grouped into daily periods, but if you want to see changes made by the minute, click "Show more detailed revisions" at the bottom of the revisions panel. You can see which collaborator made each change in a group document. Of course, the slightly less elegant Undo and Redo functions are always available as well!

Back to your masterpiece in progress: The Declaration of Independence. Michelle is ready for a second opinion of what she's done.

She knows Barack is a master orator, so she knows he's going to have some good input.

Look up in the upper right corner. See the blue button that says Share? Click on that. It's going to open up several different sharing options.

There's a few ways to share it:
1. Type their email address and let Google do the rest.
2. Manually (covered below).

Share with others   Get shareable link GD

People

Enter names or email addresses.   ✏ ▾

Done   Advanced

When you email someone, you can also manage exactly what they can do. Click that little pencil icon. By default, it will say they can edit the doc. You can change it so they can only comment on the doc, or they can only view the doc:

You can also hit advance at the bottom of the share menu, and have a few more features—such as disabling print:

But let's say you don't want to email the first man. Let's say you just want to give him a link—that way he doesn't need to use his Google account to open it. To do that, follow the steps above, but in the upper corner of the box, click "Get shareable link."

Get shareable link ⊖

Once you click that, it will give you a sharable link—it even copies the link so if you hit CTRL-V (or right-click paste) you can paste that link anywhere you want.

If you click on can view, it will give you a drop-down menu with more features. It looks sort of like the other drop-down menu above, but there's an option that says "more."

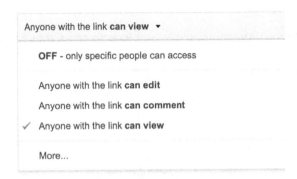

When you click on "More," it gives you a few extra features—such as making the document public in search engines so anyone can find it.

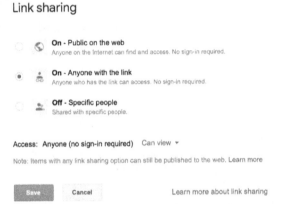

You can turn sharing off at any time, by hitting the "Share" button; once it's turned off, anyone who goes to that link—even if they've been there before—won't be able to see it. If you've emailed a person, they are still a viewer until you remove them.

If you have a person who really hates Google Docs and refuses to view your document in anything but Word, Google Docs allows you to export your work to a Word Document so you don't have to do all of the copying and font processing yourself. Just click on file > download as > Word; there's a whole host of other exports here as well.

Download as ▶	Microsoft Word (.docx)
Email as attachment	OpenDocument Format (.odt)
Version history ▶	Rich Text Format (.rtf)
	PDF Document (.pdf)
Rename	Plain Text (.txt)
Move to	
Move to trash	Web Page (.html, zipped)
	EPUB Publication (.epub)

Editing and Collaborating with Others
Let's pretend for a moment the first man is in the document and he's ready to make some changes and add some notes.

As he goes through the document, he's going to make some notes. There are a few ways to do it; the easiest way is to right-click and select "Comment."

You can also get this, by selecting Insert on the toolbar, and Comment:

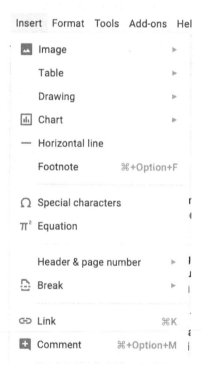

Either of these will bring up the comment box. Add your comment, and select the blue comment box when you are ready to post it. When you add a comment (or make a change), it's in real-time; that means if the person who is collaborating with you has the document open, they can actually watch you make the edits and add the comments.

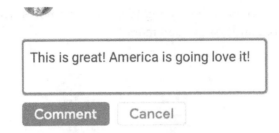

If you have multiple people working on the doc, you can type "@" and see a list of people you can mention; if you mention them, Google will notify them so they can add a reply to your comment.

Once the comment is posted, it will show up on the side of Google Docs.

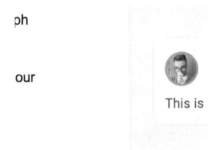

You can delete or edit the comment by clicking on those three little dots on the side of the box:

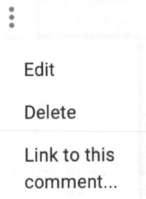

Edit

Delete

Link to this comment...

The person on the other end will be able to resolve the comment (that makes it disappear, but they can undo it).

Or they can reply to it.

When others are editing a doc I created, my personal preference is to tell them to edit with suggestions. This lets me see the changes they have made. You can turn it on by clicking on the pencil icon in the menu, and selecting "Suggesting."

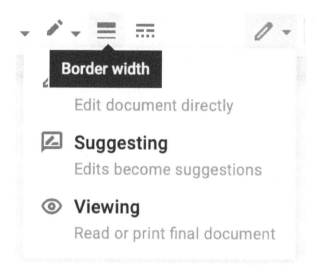

Now when they edit the doc, it will show up as a different color.

If you click on what they changed, you can accept the change with the check mark, or ignore it with the X. You can also ask questions about it and they can reply.

To see all the versions of a document, go to "file" and see versions.

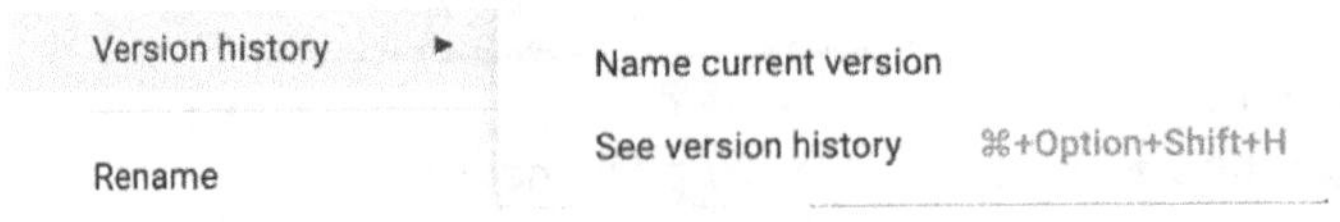

| Version history | ▶ | Name current version | |
| Rename | | See version history | ⌘+Option+Shift+H |

If there is going to be a lot of versions, then one suggestion is to name each one—which you can do here.

When you click "See version history", you'll get a list of all the versions. Clicking on any one of them will bring up that version. You can view it, or even restore it.

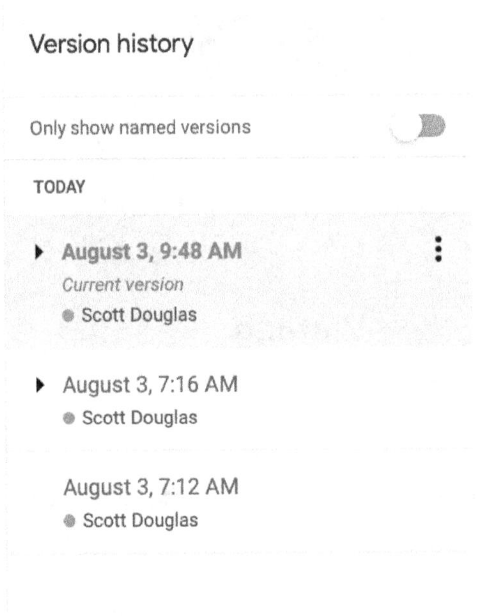

Version history

Only show named versions

TODAY

▶ **August 3, 9:48 AM**
Current version
● Scott Douglas

▶ August 3, 7:16 AM
● Scott Douglas

August 3, 7:12 AM
● Scott Douglas

To get back to the document, just hit the back button in the menu (not the browser back button):

← Today, 9:48 AM

[5]

BEYOND THE BASICS

This chapter will cover:
- Printing
- Adding photos
- Adding tables
- Adding spreadsheets
- Adding a table of contents
- Templates

Printing From the Cloud

Michelle's pretty happy with her declaration, but she's still a little old school—she likes to read through her work the old fashion way with that little thing called paper. So, she obviously needs to print it.

You probably can guess that you do this a way you are familiar with: File > Print.

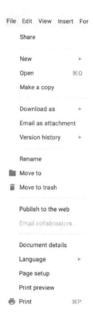

From here, it gets a little...complicated. Printing is not something Google Docs excels at.

You have two main options:

Save it to your computer and then print it from your computer.

Add your computer to Google
If you want to add your computer to Google Cloud print, then click the link.

It will walk you through the steps. The steps change depending on the kind of printer you have. It's not rocket science, but you'll need to pay attention to details.

If you want to skip the fuss there's a longer, but less hassle, way: export as a PDF, open the PDF on your computer, print it from your computer. Because you already have a printer on your computer, it will show up when you do File > Print.

Adding Photos to Google Docs

Okay, so you've printed it, you've agreed the text is where you want it to be by collaborating with others—now you want to jazz it up.

Google Docs works just like any other word processor. You can add in images wherever you want, either by copying and pasting, or by adding them in from Insert > Image.

Just find a place where you want to add an image. If you have found the image online and copied it, then just do CTRL-V, and it will be added in.

If you have the image stored on your computer, in your Google Drive, or any number of other places, then you can do one of two things. One: click Insert > Image:

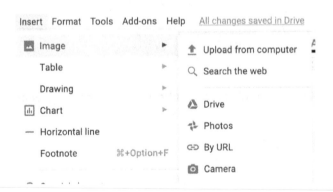

Or, two, click the Picture icon in the toolbar:

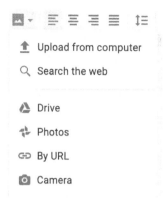

If you simply want to add the image from your computer, then choose "Upload from computer" and find it on your computer. You can also search the web for the file, paste a link to the file, or, if you are using a device that supports it, use the computer's built-in camera to add an image.

Once the image is in your document, click on it. You'll see little blue squares around it—and a small blue dot:

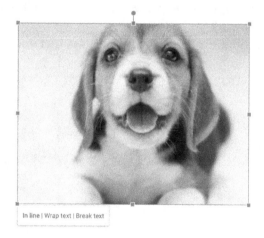

Clicking on these lets you resize the image; clicking on the dot will let you rotate the image. You can also choose how the text communicates with the image. By default, it will be Inline—that means the text will go above and below it. "Wrap text" will mean the text will go on all sides of it. "Break text" lets you put a margin around the text—if you want a little white space, for example.

If you right-click, you'll also see some extra options for the image:

Most options you probably understand. "Alt text" is handy if you'll be publishing this online—it is text that shows if the text can't be seen; you are basically describing the image.

Clicking on "Image options" will bring up even more options:

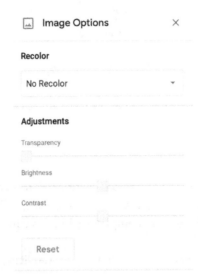

Here you can make it brighter, for example; you can also make it semi-transparent—which is great if you will be using it as a watermark.

If you change your mind about the image, you can delete it or you can just click "Replace image" when you click on it:

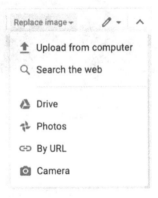

Getting Really Fancy

We have photos. It's looking snazzy, right?! Now let's dig in deeper.

Next, we are going to learn how to add in tables and spreadsheets. This might not be for everyone, but it's still good to know.

First, let's see how to do this the manual way. This is a good option if you don't have a lot of data you are working with—let's pretend here that you want to show the week's lunch menu.

Go to "Insert" on the toolbar and "Table":

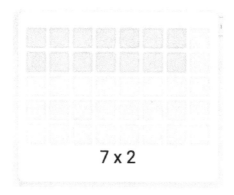

Insert Format Tools Add-ons Help   All changes sav

   🖼 Image   ▸   ▾   18   ▾   B
      Table   ▸
      Drawing   ▸
   📊 Chart   ▸
   — Horizontal line   1 x 1
      Footnote   ⌘+Option+F

From here, you'll drag the number of boxes based on how big you want your table to be. This is a lunch menu, and I'm going to make it seven days with two rows.

7 x 2

It will show up blank:

Next, I'll add in my menu. I'm personally excited for Saturday, where lunch will be a bag of Doritos—I really put a lot of effort into that lunch!

Sunday	Monday	Tuesday	Wednesday	Thursday	Friday	Saturday
Green eggs and ham	Lobster	Hamburger	Lambchops	Fish & Chips	FREE DAY	Bag of doritos

That table is nice, but it doesn't really visually illustrate anything. Next, I'm going to change the color of the top row so it stands out a bit more. Highlight that entire top row:

Sunday	Monday	Tuesday	Wednesday	Thursday	Friday	Saturday

Next, right-click, which will bring up your "Table" menu. Select "Table properties." This kind of sounds like the properties for the entire table, but because we highlighted and then right-clicked, it will only change the style of the row highlighted (if we had right-clicked without highlighting, it would have changed everything).

Merge cells

Distribute rows
Distribute columns

Table properties

Select all matching text
Update 'Normal text' to match

There's a lot of properties here, but the one we want for this row is "Cell background color":

Once you change the background, click "OK" and the table will look similar to the below:

Sunday	Monday	Tuesday	Wednesday	Thursday	Friday	Saturday
Green eggs and ham	Lobster	Hamburger	Lambchops	Fish & Chips	FREE DAY	Bag of doritos

You can also highlight one row and change the color. I'll change Friday because it's a free day and I want it to stand out more.

Let's pretend we don't want cow meat this week—we want two days of lobster! Delete "hamburger," highlight both the Monday and Tuesday boxes, right-click, and select "merge cells":

Merge cells

Distribute rows

The cell is now one box:

Sunday	Monday	Tuesday	Wednesday	Thursday	Friday	Saturday
Green eggs and ham	Lobster		Lambchops	Fish & Chips	FREE DAY	Bag of doritos

Now, let's make that menu a little taller. Right-click, "select table properties," and check off "Minimum row height." I'll make it one inch. This means if the text is longer, it could be more than 1 inch, but it will be at least one inch:

Dimensions (inches)

☐ Column width

☑ Minimum row height   1

Cell padding   0.069

Table alignment

Center ▾

Left indent (inches)   0

Sunday	Monday	Tuesday	Wednesday	Thursday	Friday	Saturday
Green eggs and ham	Lobster		Lambchops	Fish & Chips	FREE DAY	Bag of doritos

We almost have the menu where we want it, but there's still a little work to be done. Let's make the cells show the text in the middle of the cell. Go to "Table properties" and under "Cell Vertical Alignment," select "middle":

Cell vertical alignment

Top

Middle

Bottom

Now everything is evenly aligned in the middle:

Sunday	Monday	Tuesday	Wednesday	Thursday	Friday	Saturday
Green eggs and ham	Lobster		Lambchops	Fish & Chips	FREE DAY	Bag of doritos

Right now, all the columns are the same width. You can make the table larger by dragging either end of the table:

Sunday	Monday	Tuesday	Wednesday	Thursday	Friday	Saturday
Green eggs and ham	Lobster		Lambchops	Fish & Chips	FREE DAY	Bag of doritos

How to insert spreadsheets from Google Sheet

Google Docs integrates all things Google into it. Let's take that to heart and look at another Google app quickly: Google Sheets.

Go ahead and go back to drive.google.com and create a new document—this time a spreadsheet (hint: click the new button and then select spreadsheet)

In a flash you have a spreadsheet in the cloud. All the menus are pretty similar to Google Docs, and you enter text the same way.

For this example, I'm going to use a library database that's already been created. Let's pretend I want to copy some of it (though I could also do all of it) into my Google Doc. I just need to highlight what I want to copy, then either right-click and choose "copy" or do CTRL-C on the keyboard.

Next, I'll go back into my Google Doc and hit CTRL-V on the keyboard to paste it. It's going to ask us if we want to paste it in Linked or unlinked:

Paste table

◉ Link to spreadsheet
   Only editors can update the table. Collaborators can see a link to
   the source spreadsheet.

○ Paste unlinked

Learn more   Cancel   Paste

What's the difference? Linked lets a person go to that original spreadsheet—they can view other rows and make changes. Unlinked pastes it in as a new table and if you make changes to the spreadsheet, it won't show up in your Google Doc.

I'm going to pick Linked. It will paste in and look pretty...basic:

A brief history of time	Stephen W. Hawking	Hawking, Stephe n W.	Bantam Books		Astrono my		198	QB981 .H377 1988
A Career as an Electrician	Daniel E. Harmon	Harmo n, Daniel E.	The Rosen Publish ing Group, Inc	2010	Juvenil e Nonficti on		80	TK159 .H37 2011
A Child's Garden of Verses	Robert Louis Stevenson	Steven son, Robert Louis	Chronic le Books	1989	Juvenil e Nonficti on		30	PR548 9 .C5 1989
A Concise Guide to Technical Communication	Laura J. Gurak, John M. Lannon	Gurak, Laura J.	Pearso n/Long man	2004	Techno logy & Engine ering		17	T10.5 .G83 2004
A Concise Public Speaking Handbook	Steven A. Beebe, Susan J. Beebe	Beebe, Steven A.	Allyn & Bacon		Perfor ming Arts		292	PN412 9.15 .B42 2012
					Techno			TK786

Just like the table we created earlier, however, you can go in and create all sorts of styles for it. For example, I chose "table property" and changed the background color for the first two rows:

A brief history of time	Stephen W. Hawking	Hawking, Stephe n W.	Bantam Books		Astrono my		198	QB981 .H377 1988
A Career as an Electrician	Daniel E. Harmon	Harmo n, Daniel E.	The Rosen Publish ing Group, Inc	2010	Juvenil e Nonficti on		80	TK159 .H37 2011
A Child's Garden of Verses	Robert Louis Stevenson	Steven son, Robert Louis	Chronic le Books	1989	Juvenil e Nonficti on		30	PR548 9 .C5 1989
		Gurak,	Pearso		Techno logy &			T10.5

These changes don't show up in the original spreadsheet.

So let's pretend that you also linked your sheet into Google Docs. If you click on the link button in the upper corner, then you'll get new options:

You can unlink the document, for example, or open it. If sharing is not turned on, the other person won't be able to access it.

There's a Template for that

Once you know your way around Google Docs, you can save time by using one of the pre-created Google Templates for Docs. To use one, go to drive.google.com and create a Google Doc—but instead of blank, select from template.

A new window is going to open with all of your options. Unlike Word and Pages, Google isn't huge on templates, but they do allow others to add templates, and you can find plenty of others by doing a quick Google search for Google Docs templates.

Table of Contents

One useful feature is the table of contents. This would more commonly be used in a book or long-form document. You hopefully won't use it to share a love letter with your wife, but you might want to use it if you are using Google Docs for a dissertation.

You can see/add the table of contents by going to Insert > Table of contents. You can do it either with or without the page numbers:

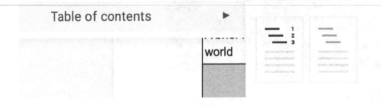

If you don't see your table of contents after adding it, there's likely a good reason: you haven't added any headings to the Doc.

Click on Normal text from your drop down. See all the different options?

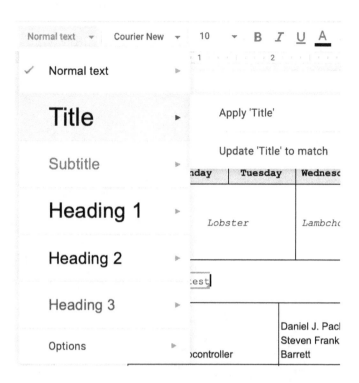

If this were a book, then "Title" would be the title on the first page. "Heading 1" would be the chapter title, "Heading 2" and "Heading 3" would be sections within that chapter.

For each one you can select "Update 'Title' to match." Let's say "Title" changes the text to size 24 but you want it to be size 36. If you change your text to size 36, then highlight it and select "Title" and update it. Then, every time you add a new Title in the doc (not other docs) it will update it to that style.

If you want it to apply to every doc going forward, then go to "Options" in that same section and select "Save as my default styles":

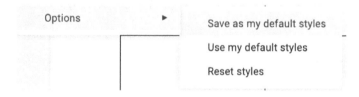

[5]

THIS AND THAT

This chapter will cover:
- Google Docs menus

In this section, I'll cover some final things you need to know about Google Docs. This isn't comprehensive—I'm not going to cover Script Editor, for example, because the point is to keep things simple and show you the features you'll most likely be using.

File menu

We've covered all the important things in the file menu, but there's one thing of note: File > Language:

By default, it will be in English; that means if you start typing a document in Spanish, then you'll see all kinds of grammatical errors. Changing the language adds in a new dictionary so it doesn't think you are just typing gibberish.

View Menu

There are two things I'll point out under the View menu. First, Print layout. By default, it's checked off. Clicking it will show the document in a long scroll view—so no page breaks:

Print layout

"Show document online" will bring up a side panel to show all the headers in your document:

Insert Menu

If you want to add a header (such as every page has your last name on top), or add in page number, then head to "Insert" and "Header & page number."

Insert > Break will add in a page break. By default, Google does this automatically, but if you are doing a new section that you want on a new page, then you can do it manually here:

Insert > Special characters is where you can grab symbols like the © sign:

Ω Special characters

Insert > Bookmark is helpful in longer documents. You can create bookmark links, so whenever you are referencing something, you can send them right to that section so they don't have to scroll to find it:

Bookmark

Tools Menu
The tools menu is where you'll find Spell checker and word count.

Tools   Add-ons   Help   All changes saved in Drive

Spelling and grammar   ►

Word count   ⌘+Shift+C

You can also see the built in dictionary and where you can translate the document into another language. I should note here that this is obviously a computer translation, so don't expect perfection.

Dictionary   ⌘+Shift+Y

Translate document

🎤 Voice typing   ⌘+Shift+S

"Explore" is helpful in research papers. It keeps you in the doc so you don't have to go to a tab to look something up:

 Explore   ⌘+Option+Shift+I

In the below example, I typed in "Stephen Colbert" and it gave me basic information about him in a side menu:

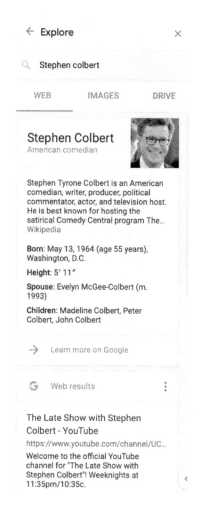

Add-ons Menu
This is where you can add on extensions if you don't go to the Google store:

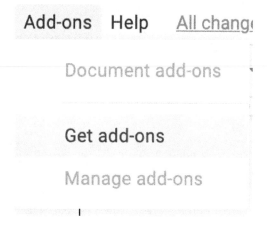

Help Menu
And finally, the help menu will let you search for common tasks, see updates to Google Docs, and even get training:

Help   All changes saved in Drive

Search the menus (Option+/)

Docs Help

Training

Updates

Report a problem

Report abuse/copyright

⌨ Keyboard shortcuts   ⌘/

[6]

GOOGLE DOCS KEYBOARD SHORTCUTS

You can see all the keyboard shortcuts in Google Docs by selecting Help > Keyboard shortcuts. For your reference, below are some of the most common ones you'll use.

Common actions

Copy	Ctrl + c
Cut	Ctrl + x
Paste	Ctrl + v
Paste without formatting	Ctrl + Shift + v
Undo	Ctrl + z
Redo	Ctrl + Shift + z
Insert or edit link	Ctrl + k
Print	Ctrl + p
Open	Ctrl + o
Find	Ctrl + f
Find and replace	Ctrl + h

Text formatting

Bold	Ctrl + b
Italicize	Ctrl + i
Underline	Ctrl + u
Strikethrough	Alt + Shift + 5
Superscript	Ctrl + .
Subscript	Ctrl + ,
Copy text formatting	Ctrl + Alt + c
Paste text formatting	Ctrl + Alt + v
Clear text formatting	Ctrl + \
Increase font size	Ctrl + Shift + >
Decrease font size	Ctrl + Shift + <

Paragraph formatting

Increase paragraph indentation	Ctrl +]
Decrease paragraph indentation	Ctrl + [
Apply normal text style	Ctrl + Alt + 0
Apply heading style [1-6]	Ctrl + Alt + [1-6]
Left align	Ctrl + Shift + l
Center align	Ctrl + Shift + e
Right align	Ctrl + Shift + r
Justify	Ctrl + Shift + j
Numbered list	Ctrl + Shift + 7

Bulleted list	Ctrl + Shift + 8

Comments

Insert comment	Ctrl + Alt + m
Open discussion thread	Ctrl + Alt + Shift + a

Menus

File menu	Alt + f
Edit menu	Alt + e
View menu	Alt + v
Insert menu	Alt + i
Format menu	Alt + o
Tools menu	Alt + t
Help menu	Alt + h

GOOGLE SHEETS

[1]

GOOGLE SHEETS CRASH COURSE

This chapter will cover:
- What is Sheets?
- Should you still use Excel?
- The Google Sheets crash course

What is Google Sheets, Anyway?

For 30-some-odd years, the world of spreadsheets has been ruled by one king: Microsoft Excel. Sure, there were far away challengers that tried to overtake the beast—I'm looking at you, Lotus 1-2-3—but none have come close to dethroning the powerful tool…until Google Sheets.

So what is Google Sheets? It's a cloud-based spreadsheet. Think Excel, but online. "But Excel is online," you say. Yes! But Google was there first, and really has the advantage over Excel in this arena. It's quicker and easier to use for collaboration.

Google Sheets is also free; Excel has monthly/yearly subscriptions.

Excel vs. Google Sheets: What's Right For Me?

If you are judging Google Sheets by mere looks, you might think it was a clone. It has tabs, it has cells, and, heck, even the formulas are largely the same!

So what is the difference?!

Let's go with the obvious one. As of this writing, you can add 5,000,000 cells to Google Sheets; Microsoft Excel? 17,179,869,184 cells.

How embarrassing, right? How on Earth can you get anything done with only 5,000,000 cells!

Kidding aside, that number does tell you one thing: Excel is the best software for large corporations managing budgets spanning dozens of years. But for the rest of us, that number really doesn't matter. A spreadsheet with 5,000,000 cells is plenty. The moment you get to cell 5,000,001 you have hopefully made it in the world and have sold your business. You now live on a private island where you ride llamas bareback on the beach. Why llamas? Because you are ridiculously wealthy and horses just seem too middleclass.

There is one other thing that's telling about that number, however. It's speed.

What do I mean by that? The reason Google limits cells is because in a cloud-based environment, the more cells you add, the slower it gets. Excel can afford crazy amounts of cells because it's locally installed. As long as you have a good computer with plenty of memory, you can have a nearly endless number of cells and not have to worry about things slowing down.

Again, most of us probably don't care about speed. We're working with smaller spreadsheets and never notice lags. But, and it's a big but, things do slow down when you start working with thousands of cells in Google, and that can be problematic for productivity.

The biggest reason people are switching to Google Sheets, however, is collaboration. Google is king when it comes to collaboration. If you are working on a budget with a group of people, then Google is hands down the way to go.

The Google Sheets Crash Course

The first three buttons are pretty straightforward: undo, redo what you have typed and print. The last one is the format painter; this lets you copy the style of one cell into another cell. To use it, click the cell you want to copy, select the format painter, and then click the cell you want to put the style in.

By default, a spreadsheet is viewed at 100%; if you are working with a larger sheet and want to see more cells on your screen, you can use this to zoom out—or also to zoom in and see less cells on your screen.

100% ▼

The next five options tell the cell what the content is. $ turns it into currency; % turns it into a percentage; the next two move the decimals forward and backward; and finally, the 123 gives you additional options to telling the cell what it is—plain text, a scientific formula, a date, etc. This is also useful if you have a number, but you want Google to treat it like plain text.

$ %   .0   .00   123 ▼

If you have used any kind of productivity software, then you should know the next two options; if you've been under a rock: this is the font and font size.

Arial   ▼   10   ▼

Next to the font is the font formatter; here you can bold, italicize, strikethrough (i.e. put a line through the middle of the text), or change the number.

B *I* S̶ <u>A</u>

The next set of options is for the cell style; you can change the fill color, the cell border, and merge cells. To merge cells, highlight the cells you want to merge and then click this option.

Justification and placement are managed in the next four options. Here you can center/right/left align, move the content to the bottom/middle/top of the cell, wrap the text (by default text will just spill over into the next cell unless you resize the cell; this option tells it to make the text go to the next line, sort of like hitting the enter key, since the enter/return key doesn't work in Sheets); and finally rotate text, which also lets you change the direction of the text.

The last set of options is to insert things into a cell. You can insert a link, comment, chart, filter, or function.

On the far side, is an up arrow. This just hides or unhides the toolbar.

[2]

GETTING STARTED WITH GOOGLE SHEETS

This chapter will cover:
- Your first Sheet
- Opening saved documents
- The basics

Okay, so how exactly do you use Google Sheets? Like everything else in the Google Suite family! The beauty of Google is once you learn one, learning others is pretty easy.

Here's a refresher: type in drive.google.com.
Once you have your Google account (hopefully you do by now), then you are all set. Repeat the step above and the browser Window should look more like the below.

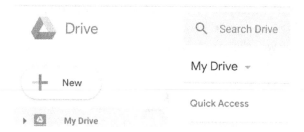

Creating Your First Sheet

Now that you have your account, let's create a document. Click on the "New" button and then hover over Google Sheets; there are two options: "Blank document" and "From a template." For now, select "From a template." I'll cover templates a little bit later.

At this point, you'll be taken to Google's Sheets editor. This is where you do the actual work. Everything is designed to function just like Excel or Numbers.

Have a look in the upper left-hand corner of your Google Sheets. You'll see a text field that says "Untitled Document." Click on that.

You will now be prompted with a box asking you to rename the document. I chose "My Glorious Google Sheet!," but you can type anything you want. When you finish, hit the enter key.

Once you do that, the top bar will change, reflecting the new name you've chosen:

My Glorious Google Sheet! in 🗀 My Drive
File   Edit   View   Insert   Format   Data   Tools   Add-ons   Help   All changes saved in Drive

Do you see the text on the right where it says, "All changes saved"? That's another awesome thing about Google Sheets:

<h2 style="text-align:center">All changes saved in Drive</h2>

In a stroke of pure brilliance, the folks at Google have decided to completely automate document saves. As you write, Google saves your project and tells you when it last did this. If you want, you can go ahead and save, but it's practically unnecessary. Google Sheets saves after you enter every new word.

Opening A Saved Document

Don't worry about accidently closing your tab. When you open it back up, Google will take you right back to your list of documents. You should see your document at the top of that list in "Quick Access."

If you are just getting started, it will also be the only sheet you see, and you can access it below the quick access

List view looks like the above—it gives the name, who the owner is, and the time it was edited. Grid view is more of a thumbnail preview of the Sheet.

Notice how "author" and "time lasted edited" is gone?

What's better? It's a preference, but if you are working with dozens of files, then Grid view probably will not be ideal unless you need to see previews.

To toggle between the two, click these icons in the upper corner:

List is the horizontal lines, and grid is the six square boxes.

The most recently viewed and edited files gets the top spot.

When you double-click on the Sheet or document you want, it'll open right up in the browser, and we can get back to writing. It's just like opening up an Excel or Numbers document on your home computer.

The Basics

Now that we've gotten our quick crash course, let's add some numbers and see how this thing works.

I'll start by adding some years; like any good spreadsheet software, Google is pretty good at guessing. If there's a pattern, then you can autofill the cells. In the example below, I've added two years: 1900 and 1901. When I highlight those two cells, there's a tiny blue box:

	A
1	Year
2	1900
3	1901

If I drag that blue box down, Google will correctly predict that I am putting years in and add one year per cell for as long as I drag:

	A
1	Year
2	1900
3	1901
4	1902
5	1903
6	1904
7	1905
8	1906
9	1907
10	1908
11	1909
12	1910
13	

For this example, I'm going to create another column that shows how many babies were born, then two fields to show the total babies and average babies born.

To get the total number, go to the cell and type "=sum(". Google will probably highlight what it thinks you want automatically, but if it doesn't, then just highlight the cells you want to add up and then hit Enter/Return:

Year	Babies Born
1900	33
1901	100
1902	4
1903	22
1904	21
1905	99
1906	73
1907	9
1908	9
1909	60
1910	81
Babies Born	=SUM
Average	SUM(B2:B12)
	Suggested based on the data.

The same method is used for averages, but you type =average(instead of sum:

Year	Babies Born
1900	33
1901	100
1902	4
1903	22
1904	21
1905	99
1906	73
1907	9
1908	9
1909	60
1910	81
Babies Born	46.45454545 ×
Average	=Average(B2:B12)

In seconds, we now know the number of babies born as well as the average for all years:

Year	Babies Born
1900	33
1901	100
1902	4
1903	22
1904	21
1905	99
1906	73
1907	9
1908	9
1909	60
1910	81
Babies Born	511
Average	46.45454545

Not happy with how it looks? You can apply basic formatting the same way you would in a Google Doc or Word Doc:

Year	Babies Born
1900	33
1901	100
1902	4
1903	22
1904	21
1905	
1906	73
1907	9
1908	9
1909	60
1910	81
Babies Born	412
Average	41.2

[3]

BEYOND THE BASICS

This chapter will cover:
- Creating charts
- Functions
- Scripts

Creating a Chart

People are visual. Numbers aren't very sexy. You need visuals to make them pop.

Before we go deeper into the fun world of functions, let's take the fun out of functions and do something fun: a chart.

I'll take the example above and create a chart that shows the babies born per year a little more visually.

To get started, I'll highlight what I want to show; in my example, only the top portion—the chart doesn't need to show the totals or averages:

	A	B
1	Year	Babies Born
2	1900	33
3	1901	100
4	1902	4
5	1903	22
6	1904	21
7	1905	99
8	1906	73
9	1907	9
10	1908	9
11	1909	60
12	1910	81
13		
14		
15	Babies Born	511
16	Average	46.45454545

Next, go to the toolbar and click the chart icon:

And just like that, we have a pretty line graph that represents our data:

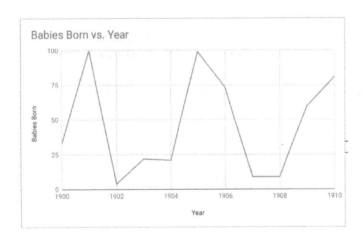

I know, I know...you're sitting there thinking: Lines! I hate lines!

Don't fret! You use the chart editor that opens a chart library to create dozens of other charts:

If you got so excited when the chart came up on your screen that you accidentally closed the chart editor, then just double click the chart and it will open back up:

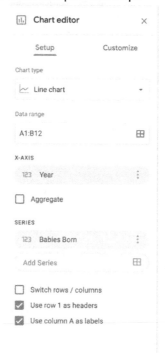

You can use this editor to change the range (you add some more rows, for example, and want them represented) or reverse the data shown—you want to show the years on the lines, not the number of babies born.

Google has its own idea of what is pretty. It's probably different from yours. You don't want a blue line! You want a red line! You hate the black text! You want green! If there's one thing Spreadsheet people are known for, it's their incredible talent for making numbers look sexy. Don't worry! You can customize almost everything here.

If you need to bring sexy back to your chart, then just go into your editor and select "Customize" right next to "Setup."

Setup   Customize

From here you can go section-to-section and change colors, fonts, and more:

⌄   Chart style

Background color   Font

⬭ ▾   Roboto   ▾

Chart border color

⬤ ▾

☐ Smooth
☐ Maximize
☐ Plot null values
☐ Compare mode

You can also change gridlines around on the bottom:

⌄   Gridlines

Vertical axis   ▾

Major gridline count   Major gridline color

Auto   ▾   Auto ▾

Minor gridline count   Minor gridline color

None   ▾

By default, Google will just stick the chart inconveniently over your data. If you click on it, you'll see a bunch of little blue boxes. That means you can either resize it (click on one and drag in/out to make it larger/smaller) or move it:

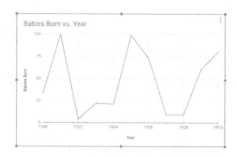

You'll also notice three little boxes in the upper right corner of the chart. That's your chart menu. Click that and you'll see several options:

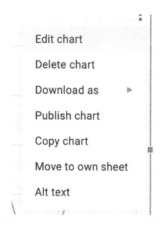

Download as is helpful if you want to insert it into emails as attachments or presentations. You can download it as an image or PDF.

You can also copy and paste the chart into other Google app—like Google Slides or Google Docs. Just click it and do CTRL+C on your keyboard to copy it, and CTRL+V to paste it.

Functionally Yours

Now that we had some fun, let's get serious and learn about functions.

What is a function exactly? Well, we already learned about two: Sum and Average. Functions are the formulas you put into cells to tell Google to calculate an equation.

There are a lot of functions. Go to your toolbar and click the function key, and you can see what I mean!

The main ones you use will be right at the top, which is helpful; below that, Google has categorized additional ones.

Because this book is meant to get you started quickly and not teach you all the features that you will never use, I won't cover every single function here. The goal is to show you how they work, so if there's one not covered here that you want to use, you'll know how.

I recommend you spend a few minutes looking at the list above and see if there's something that would be useful to what you are doing. There are hundreds of functions.

To use any of the functions in this list, go to the cell you want to show the equation in, and then click the function option and select the one you want to do; from here, select your data range. Once it's selected, hit return/enter.

If you decide later that you need to edit the function, go to the upper left corner—just under the tool bar. See the fx? When you select a cell with a function, it will show up here. Click in there, and then update the range that you want.

That's also the same place you go to edit anything in a cell—function or no function.

So Many Functions...That I Don't Want

Google Sheets has a lot of functions. It's overwhelming, but it doesn't have everything. If you become a power spreadsheets user, you might find it would be helpful to do something that there is no function for.

That doesn't mean you can't do it. It's just a little more involved. There are many more things you can do by creating a script. Scripts let you basically program your own function.

Scripts can be found by going to Tools > Scripts Editor.

This is going to launch a separate Google app for creating a script:

Below is an example of what a script might look like:

```
var ss = SpreadsheetApp.getActiveSpreadsheet();
var sheet = ss.getSheets()[0];

// The size of the two-dimensional array must match the size of
var values = [
  [ "2.000", "1,000,000", "$2.99" ]
];

var range = sheet.getRange("B2:D2");
range.setValues(values);
```

Once you have your script written, go to Publish > Deploy as Sheets add-on:

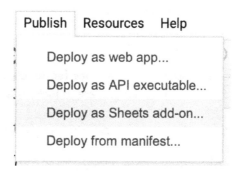

The topic of scripts is much too complicated for this book, but there are plenty of resources both in the Scripts app and online if this is an arena you'd like to dig deeper into later.

[4]

SHARING IS CARING

This chapter will cover:
- Sharing your sheet
- Editing and collaborating sheets
- Protecting sheets
- Data validation

Sharing Your Sheet

Now that you know your way around, you're ready for feedback from others.

If you know how to share a Google Doc, then you are in luck! Sharing Sheets is the same. Need a refresher?

Look up in the upper right corner. See the blue button that says Share? Click on that. It's going to open up several different sharing options.

When you click on that, a share box opens up, and you get a bunch of different options.

There's a few ways to share it:
1. Type their email address and let Google do the rest.
2. Manually (covered below).

Share with others   Get shareable link ⊝

People

Enter names or email addresses...   ✏ ▾

    Done   Advanced

When you email someone, you can also manage exactly what they can do. Click that little pencil icon. By default, it will say they can edit the doc. You can change it so they can only comment on the doc, or they can only view the doc:

You can also hit advance at the bottom of the share menu, and have a few more features—such as disabling print:

But let's say you don't want to email the first man. Let's say you just want to give him a link—that way he doesn't need to use his Google account to open it. To do that, follow the steps above, but in the upper corner of the box, click "Get shareable link."

Once you click that, it will give you a sharable link—it even copies the link so if you hit CTRL-V (or right-click paste) you can paste that link anywhere you want.

If you click on can view, it will give you a drop-down menu with more features. It looks sort of like the other drop-down menu above, but there's an option that says "more."

Anyone with the link **can view** ▾

>
> **OFF** - only specific people can access
>
> Anyone with the link **can edit**
>
> Anyone with the link **can comment**
>
> ✓ Anyone with the link **can view**
>
> More...

When you click on "More," it gives you a few extra features—such as making the document public in search engines so anyone can find it.

Link sharing

> ◯ 🌐 **On - Public on the web**
>   Anyone on the Internet can find and access. No sign-in required.
>
> ⦿ 👥 **On - Anyone with the link**
>   Anyone who has the link can access. No sign-in required.
>
> ◯ 👤 **Off - Specific people**
>   Shared with specific people.

Access: Anyone (no sign-in required)   Can view ▾

Note: Items with any link sharing option can still be published to the web. Learn more

Save   Cancel   Learn more about link sharing

You can turn sharing off at any time, by hitting the "Share" button; once it's turned off, anyone who goes to that link—even if they've been there before—won't be able to see it. If you've emailed a person, they are still a viewer until you remove them.

If you have a person who really hates Google Sheets and refuses to view your document in anything but Word, Google Docs allows you to export your work to a Excel Document so you don't have to do all of the copying and font processing yourself. Just click on file --> download as --> Excel; there's a whole host of other exports here as well.

Editing and Collaborating With Others
The easiest way to make comments in a spreadsheet is to right-click and select Comment.

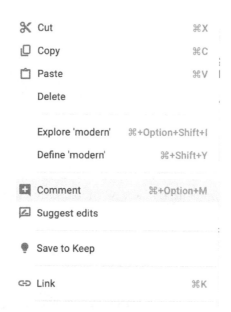

You can also get this, by selecting Insert on the toolbar, and Comment.

Either of these will bring up the comment box. Add your comment, and select the blue comment box when you are ready to post it. When you add a comment (or make a change), it's in real-time; that means if the person who is collaborating with you has the document open, they can actually watch you make the edits and add the comments.

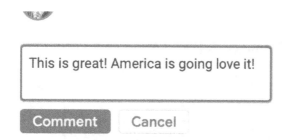

If you have multiple people working on the doc, you can type "@" and see a list of people you can mention; if you mention them, Google will notify them so they can add a reply to your comment.

Once the comments in, it will show up on the side of Google Sheets.

ph

our

This is

You can delete or edit the comment, by click on those three little dots on the side of the box.

Edit

Delete

Link to this comment...

The person on the other end will be able to resolve the comment (that makes it disappear, but they can undo it)

Or they can reply to it.
To see all the versions of a document, go to file and see versions.

If there's going to be a lot of versions, then one suggestion is to name each one—which you can do here.

When you click See version history, you'll get a list of all the versions. Clicking on anyone will bring up that version. You can view it, or even restore it.

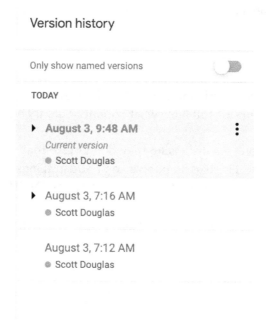

To get back to the document, just hit the back button in the menu (not the browser back button).

← Today, 9:48 AM

Protect a Spreadsheet
Google Sheets has an extra layer of protection not seen in Google Docs. To apply it, go to Tools > Protect Sheet.

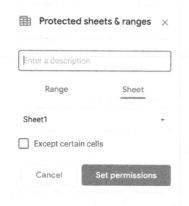

From here you can do several things:
Give it a description – Why does it need a description? Because you can create several difference protections.
Select the range.

Set permissions – you can, for example, give one person the ability to make changes and another the ability only to see it.

Data Validation

Let's say you give someone permission to edit the sheet and they add in something wrong; that error messes up the entire spreadsheet! Now what? Spent hours trying to figure out the mess they made, right?

Sure, why not! But why don't we make sure they don't make that mess to begin with!

Data validation let's you add in rules so people can't add in things incorrectly. For example, let's say someone doesn't know the answer so they just put in "?" or "N/A." You can set up a rule that forces them only to use a number.

To add one in, highlight the cells you want to apply it to and then go to Data > Data validation. This brings up the option box.

From here you need to set your rule (or criteria).

My rule is the data here needs to be a number between 0 and 101. If you want to get really fancy, you can add in a custom formula.

Next, you need to say what happens if they break the rule. Do you want to outright reject it or just give them a warning. In my case, I'm all about rejection. But I'm a nice guy too, so I'm going to tell them why I'm rejecting them.

On invalid data: ○ Show warning   ● Reject input

Appearance: ☑ Show validation help text:

> Numbers Only!   Reset

Now if someone tries to add anything but a number, then tell get this message.

There was a problem   ✕

Numbers Only!

OK

[5]

THIS AND THAT

This chapter will cover:
- Surveys
- Google Sheets menus

Survey's Into Data

One area Google Sheets has Excel and other programs beat is it's survey integration.

Using Google Forms to create a survey, you can have all the answers go right into a Google Sheet so you can collate your results.

To get started go to Insert > Forms.

This is going to launch a separate tab with the Google Forms application.

I'm going to make this survey simple, but if you want to jazz it up, there's all kinds of options for adding photos and changing styles around. Use the menu on the right side for those options.

For my survey, I'm going to make it a drop-down survey. You can change the question type by selecting the drop down to the right side of the question name; you can have as many types as you want in the survey—for example, question one could be multiple choice and question two could be a drop down.

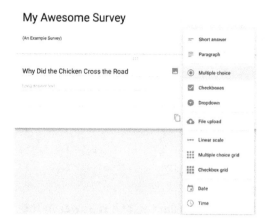

This changes our answers to editable fields. Right now, it has room for two questions. As soon as I stop typing in the second answer, a slot will be added for a third question.

More answer slots are added with each question.

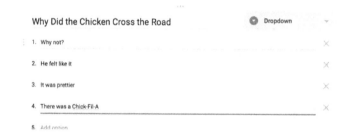

When you are done, click the "Send Form" button in the upper right corner:

I don't want to send the form to anyone—I want it to be a link. So, I'm going to click the link icon next to the email one (it's the middle one).

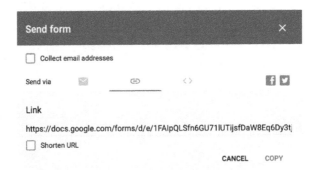

When someone goes to my survey, it will look a little bit different from the one that was in the editor because all the menu fields are gone.

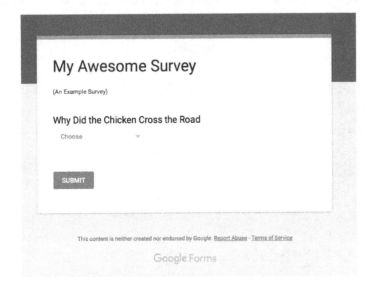

Once they click submit, they'll see a confirmation. You can make this a custom confirmation or use the default Google one.

Now that you have a response, go back to your Sheet and you'll see a new tab has been added on the bottom of the sheet for form responses.

Click that and you can see what the person answered.

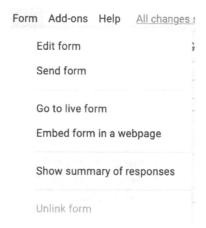

If you need to make changes to it, just go to Form from your menu bar.

Form	Add-ons	Help	All changes
	Edit form		
	Send form		
	Go to live form		
	Embed form in a webpage		
	Show summary of responses		
	Unlink form		

If you have multiple forms, then this option will not show on your menu bar unless you are inside that form tab. So if you don't see the option, then click the tab for the Form responses and then it will appear in the menu.

If you decide to delete the form, it's a little different from a normal tab. A normal tab, you right-click on the tab and hit delete, it will tell you that you can't. You have to unlink it first. How? Easy!

Right-click on the form tab you want to unlink and select Unlink form.

Once it's unlinked, you'll be able to delete it, by right-clicking and selecting delete.

This and That

By now, you should be have a really good idea how Google Sheets work. Before leaving you, I'll cover a few more features that you should know about.

By default, Google will base the Sheet on your Google Account; if your Google Account thinks you live in Spain, then that's how the Sheet is set up.

You can change this by going to File > Spreadsheet settings.

Spreadsheet settings

This is helpful if you, for example, live in the United States, but happen to be working on a Sheet for someone who lives in the UK. You can change the settings, so it shows as pounds instead of dollars.

When you start working on large documents, it gets difficult to find things. Imagine you have 100,000 cells and you have to find the one with the number "12a?b44." Good luck with that! Fortunately for you, there's something called "Find and Replace" under the Edit menu.

Not only does it find the cell you are looking for, but it let's you replace it with something else. For example, I can tell it to find every example of "California" and replace it with "CA."
Another handy feature if you have lots of rows is the freeze option. That's under View > Freeze.

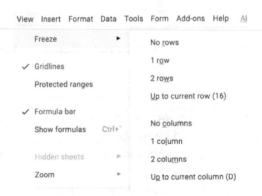

What exactly is freeze? Typically, you have a top row that is sort of like a menu. It tells the view what is in each column. And then you have the first column that has something else descriptive—such as dates. Now imagine you have 10,000 rows. You're on row 2079, column AA. You can't remember what that row stands for. If you had freeze row enabled, then that top menu (or side column) would be frozen, so no matter where you are, you always see it.

If you are editing a lot of formulas, go to View and check off "Show formulas." This will show you the formula instead of the answer. It's helpful for editing formulas.

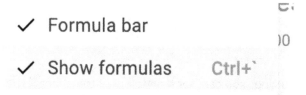

If you are in the middle of a large sheet and need to add in a row in the middle, then select the row you want to add it to, then go to Insert > and select Row above, Row below, or anywhere else you want it.

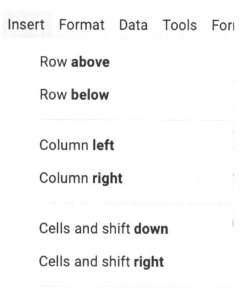

Insert > Checkbox is useful if you have people viewing it and you want them to confirm that they see something.

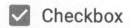

If you want to add a new tab to the bottom of your sheet, you can either click the + in the lower left corner of the sheet, or go to Insert > New sheet. To delete the sheet, right-click the tab and select delete.

New sheet   Shift+F11

You learned earlier about setting rules to a Sheet with data validation. You can do something similar with format. This is found in Format > Conditional formatting.

Conditional formatting

With conditional formatting, you can, for example, tell the sheet if the cell is empty, it's green, but if it has content, then it's blue. You can do it for run cell, or highlight multiple cells to do it for several.

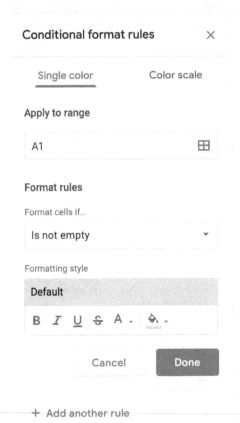

If you are working with a large sheet, and want to make sure there's no duplicate content, then highlight the range, then select Data > Remove duplicates. This will go through the range and remove anything that's the same.

Remove duplicates   New

Macros are a bit complex, they help you create sequences to automate certain tasks. I won't cover them here, but if you want to use them, it's under Tools > Macro.

Also under tools is Notification rules.

Notification rules

This is what you will use if you want to be notification when someone edits your document, or adds something to your survey. You can either be emailed immediately or once a day.

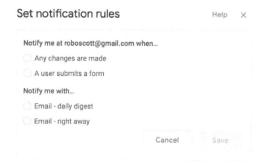

There's still a lot to learn, but I hope you now have the understanding and using Sheets comfortably.

If you find yourself copying a lot of formulas and getting errors, try pasting only the values. That means it will only copy the number and not the actual formula. You can do this by pressing CTRL+Shift+V, or by going to Edit > Paste special.

[6]

GOOGLE SHEETS KEYBOARD SHORTCUTS

You can see all the keyboard shortcuts in Google Sheets by selecting Help > Keyboard shortcuts. For your reference, below are some of the most common ones you'll use.

Common actions

Select column	Ctrl + Space
Select row	Shift + Space
Select all	Ctrl + a
Undo	Ctrl + z
Redo	Ctrl + y
Find	Ctrl + f
Find and replace	Ctrl + h
Fill range	Ctrl + Enter
Fill down	Ctrl + d
Fill right	Ctrl + r
Copy	Ctrl + c
Cut	Ctrl + x
Paste	Ctrl + v
Paste values only	Ctrl + Shift + v

Format cells

Bold	Ctrl + b
Underline	Ctrl + u
Italic	Ctrl + i
Strikethrough	Alt + Shift + 5
Center align	Ctrl + Shift + e
Left align	Ctrl + Shift + l
Right align	Ctrl + Shift + r
Apply top border	Alt + Shift + 1
Apply right border	Alt + Shift + 2
Apply bottom border	Alt + Shift + 3
Apply left border	Alt + Shift + 4
Remove borders	Alt + Shift + 6
Apply outer border	Alt + Shift + 7
Insert link	Ctrl + k
Insert time	Ctrl + Shift + ;
Insert date	Ctrl + ;

Insert date and time	Ctrl + Alt + Shift + ;
Format as decimal	Ctrl + Shift + 1
Format as time	Ctrl + Shift + 2
Format as date	Ctrl + Shift + 3
Format as currency	Ctrl + Shift + 4
Format as percentage	Ctrl + Shift + 5
Format as exponent	Ctrl + Shift + 6
Clear formatting	Ctrl + \

Use formulas

Show all formulas	Ctrl + ~
Insert array formula	Ctrl + Shift + Enter
Collapse an expanded array formula	Ctrl + e
Show/hide formula help *(when entering a formula)*	Shift + F1
Full/compact formula help *(when entering a formula)*	F1
Absolute/relative references *(when entering a formula)*	F4
Toggle formula result previews *(when entering a formula)*	F9
Resize formula bar *(move up or down)*	Ctrl + Up / Ctrl + Down

GOOGLE SLIDES

[1]

GOOGLE SLIDES CRASH COURSE

This chapter will cover:
- What is Slides?
- Slides crash course

How many times do you work on a presentation that you will get absolutely no feedback on and want no help?

Maybe you're the type that likes to whip something up and have no practice or feedback at all? Most of us are the former. Before we stand in front of a group of people, we want to make sure we're as polished as possible.

The problem is PowerPoint wasn't built like that. It was built as a desktop program that one person would use at a time.

Google realized the problem and seized the opportunity when they launched Google Slides over ten years ago.

Google Slides is a cloud-based presentation editor that can replace PowerPoint or Keynote.

If you'd like to get the most out of the software, then let's get started!

Slides Crash Course

There's a lot to cover. In the next section, we'll start from scratch with a blank presentation, but before we get there, I'm going to quickly go over the main tool bars.

This is going to be a quick overview, so if there's something you don't understand, that's okay—I'll cover it in more detail later in the book.

The first button is one you'll probably use a lot. That's how you add a new Slide. When you click the drop down, you can see all the predefined layouts. Click it and the layout will be added (hint: you'll be able to change it later).

Next to that is the undo, redo, and print icon. The last option is the format painter. This copies one style to another—for example, you want to copy the font color and size of one text, to another text. To use it, just highlight the style you want to copy, select the icon, then click the text you want to copy it to.

Next is the zoom icon. This lets you zoom in or out, so you can see more or less of your slide.

The insert options are next. The first icon (the cursor) lets you select an object, the next lets you add a text box, next to that is the insert image option, and finally, the last, insert a shape.

There's one final insert option: line. There are a couple different lines you can when you select the drop down. The scribble line is if you want to draw the line freehand.

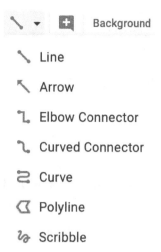

Because Google Slides is so collaborative, you'll probably use the next button a lot: the comment option. This lets you add comments to any slide or text.

The background button let's you add an image or color to your slide background.

Background

The layout option looks similar to the Add Slide button. This lets you change the layout of the selected slide.

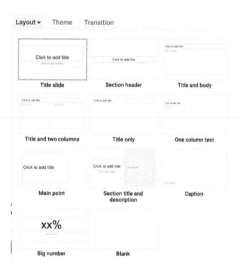

The theme button is similar to layout, but instead of text, it's changing the style of the slide—adding a background image, for example.

Theme

Finally, the Transition button is where you tell Google Slides what to do whenever you go to the next slide.

Transition

Hanging out at the far right side is the menu hide button. Use this to toggle between hide and unhide.

Over on the far left side, the side menu has three options: calendar, Google keep, and tasks. These are sort of mini apps. They don't change your slide—they just help you keep notes and pull up dates.

[2]

GETTING STARTED WITH GOOGLE SLIDES

This chapter will cover:
- Creating your first slide
- The basics

Now that we know the basics, let's dig in and see how to use the features in practice. To get started, head to drive.google.com (create an account if you haven't already) and click the create new button, then Google Slides, and blank presentation.

Right off the bat, it probably looks a little familiar to you if you've used PowerPoint or Keynote.

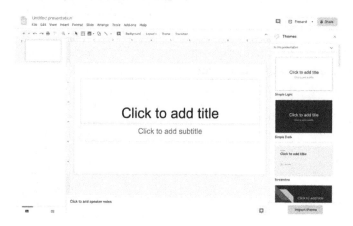

For this book, we're going to create a presentation on how to know if your friend is a monster. How many books on Google Slides, also give you valuable information on friendship?! Your welcome!

I find the best kind of learning is through actually doing something, so fill free to work on a similar presentation as you go.

First, things first: let's rename our document. Technically, this isn't required. You could give it no name and it's still going to be saving in the background. Naming it will just help you find it later.

To name it, just click once on that name area in the upper left corner and start typing. Hit enter when you are done.

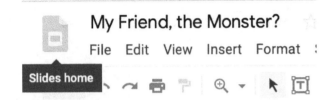

Want to rename it? Simple. Just click in that area again. Gone are the days of File > Save As. Now let's move to our first slide—the title slide—and give the presentation a name.

The 9 Steps

To Know If Your Friend Is a Monster

That's pretty straightforward, but it's also a little...boring. Let's add a fun background to it.

For this book, I went to google.com/images. That's a nice resource for pictures, but you have to keep in mind that many are copyrighted, so be mindful of what you are using—especially if the presentation is for non-instructional commercial use.

Once you have your image, you can either save it, or just copy and paste it right into your slide.

To add it, there's two methods. I prefer the second, because there's more customation to it, but I'll show you both approaches here.

For the first approach, go to your toolbar and click the Background button. From here you can either give it a solid background color, or make an image a background.

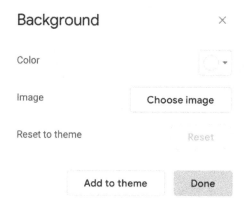

If you are just using a color, then it can work. If you are using an image, then personally I find it problematic because there's not a lot of adjustments that can be made to the image at this level. Take a look at the background below.

Not incredibly easy to see the text, right? How do we fix that? We use the second option. Either copy and paste the image onto the slide or go to Insert > Slide. This will put the image on top of the text. Not much better right? You can fix that by right-clicking the image and selecting "Send to back."

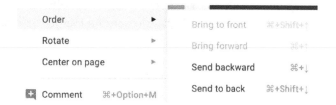

That basically makes it the same as having it as a background image, so it's still not where it needs to be. But now when you click on the image, it brings up a format menu. One option is transparency. Transparency makes the image more see through—like a watermark.

After making it a little transparent, it looks like the below image.

Better, right? But it is bigger than the slide. If you are presenting the slide, it will only show what's in the slide box, but it's much easier to work on a presentation in editor mode when it matches what the presentation will look like, so let's crop it. Right-click on the image, then select "Crop image."

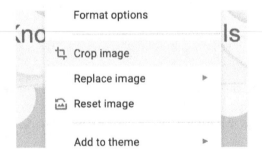

This brings up small blue boxes. Just drag those in so it fits in the slide.

Now we are ready for our next slide. There are two methods to do this. Click the + sign in the menu toolbar.

The second method is to click under the first slide and hit the enter / return button on your keyboard.

The default slide will look like the below.

You can change the layout by either right-clicking on the slide thumbnail on the left side. Or going to the menu and clicking on layout.

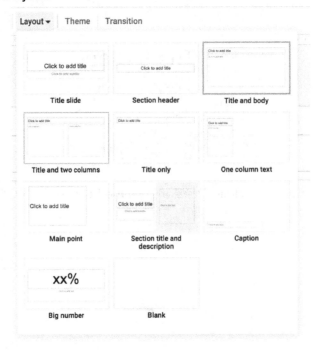

I'll change my layout to two columns.

Next, I'll add in some content.

There are two kinds of friends

Good friends   Bad friends

Awesome! Visually stunning! Let's call it a day! Don't get ahead of yourself, cowboy…there's still some work to be done here. Let's throw in some images. Again, you can either do Insert > Picture or just copy and paste it in.

Those pictures are a little…black and white—both literally and figuratively. Right-click on the image, then go format options. For this image, I'm going to check off "Reflection" to make it pop a little. This puts a shadow effect on the image.

The pictures are fine. Now let's work on the text. The header needs to be all caps. We can either type it again with all caps on, or we highlight the text, and then go to Format > Text > Capitalization > UPPERCASE.

Do the same to the text under that, but for that make it Title Case. Next we want to center align it. You may not see this option if you have the format menu open, but it's still there. To the far right of the toolbar, you'll see three dots. Click that, and it will bring up the hidden menu. From here you can center align it.

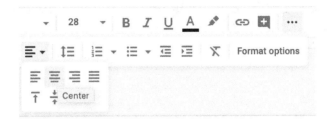

We are also going to change the text color using the button with the A and black line under it.

Now everything will be centered, and a different color.

That's still not very colorful. We could add an image to the background like the first slide, but images as backgrounds can make things look too busy. So let's do a solid color. Click Background from the toolbar and then change it to the one you want.

That's better. But I want the slide header to pop out more. I'm going to put a separate background behind it. Go to the Shapes button on the menu bar and select the rectangle.

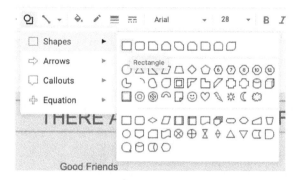

Now drag a rectangle on the upper portion of that slide. I want the box itself to pop more, so I'm also going to right-click, select Format options, and check off "Drop shadow." This gives the box a more 3D effect by putting a subtle shadow behind it.

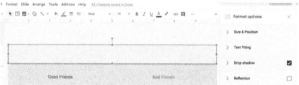

Now we just need to send the box to the back so the text is in front of it. To do that, right-click on the box and under Order select send to back. I also click the text and moved it a little higher up, so it was in the middle of the box.

Now the slide is taking shape, but let's do a few more things. Next, let's make the subtitle text come out more. Click the top box you just created and copy and paste it (CTRL+C and CTRL+V). Then move that box under the top one, right-click it, and do format options; change the color of the box so it's not the same as the other box.

After you change the color, right-click and select Order and send to the back. The text is kind of small, so let's make it bigger and then adjust it so it's more in the middle of the box. Change the font size in the menu bar; by default it's 14.

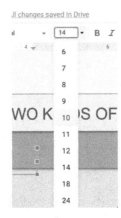

Finally, that dark grey I used doesn't really work. I'm going to make the box white. Right-click, select format options, and then change the color to white.

I want to put a line between friendship to separate the good friends from the bad. Go to the menu bar, click the line option, and select the first line. As you draw the line, hold the shift on the keyboard—that's going to make it a straight line—so it doesn't go diagonal at all.

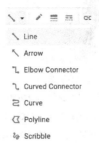

The line is going to be pretty thin; that works for some things, but here we want to beef it up. Click the line, then go to the menu bar. See the box with the lines of different weights? That's what you want. It's like a font size, but for a shape. If you don't see it, then you haven't selected the line. Click it one time.

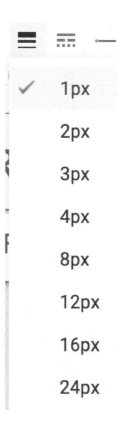

Now that the line is wider, we have everything where we want it to be.

You can create a different look for every slide, but to save yourself a lot of time, copying the slide is a lot faster. Go to the left pane where the slide thumbnails are. Right-click, and select, duplicate slides.

From here, all we have to do is take out the text we don't want and change the images.

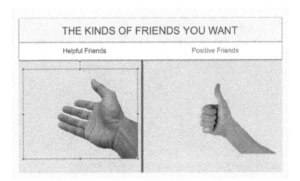

The image above feels a little off. I don't want both hands going the same direction. That's an easy fix. Select one of the images, select format options, and then under rotate, select Flip.

That's going to horizontally flip the image you've selected.

So things are going great! You have three slides! But wait! You just realized that the third slide needs to be the second slide! Now what! Easy! Just click the thumbnail of the slide in the left pane, and drag it to where you want it to go.

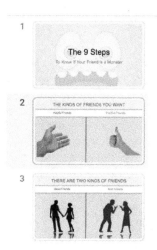

Now that you have the Slides, you need transitions between them. You won't see this in editor mode, but transitions is what happens when you are presenting a presentation between each slide—does it show a dissolve, for example.

To add in a transition, right-click on the thumbnail you want, and then select change transition.

This brings up the Transition menu; you can change one transition or apply the transition to all of the slides.

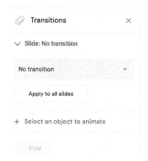

[3]

SHARING IS CARING

This chapter will cover:
- How to share
- Sharing settings
- Naming versions

Are you ready to share your slides about friends with your friends? Google Slides is a collaborative platform, so sharing is where things really come together. With sharing you can get feedback and also have others edit your slides (or you can disable editing and only get feedback)

To share, click the Share button in the upper right corner.

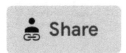

If you've used any other Google apps software, then you'll probably know what to do next—they all work exactly the same. You'll have a box to either share the Slide with specific people via email, or you can send them a link to it.

If you click on can view you'll get a drop down with varies options. If you only want people to see it, but not do anything else, for example.

If you click on Advanced, you'll have even more options—such as preventing editors from adding people or disabling copying anything in the doc.

Once people are in your document, and ready to make changes, things get a little—difficult. Unlike Google Docs where you can track changes, Google Slides doesn't have that option. If someone makes a change, there's no good visible way to see it.

You can ask them to comment instead. To do that, have them right-click and select comment. Or go to Insert > Comment:

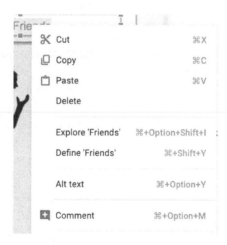

There's one final way to keep track of changes—albeit, not the ideal one. That way is to view the history. You can see the history by going to File > Version history > See version history.

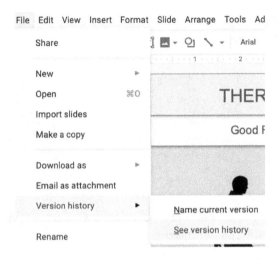

This will show you a list of changes and timestamp when they were made.

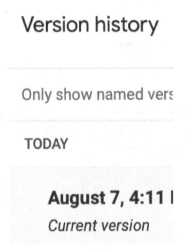

If you are using this method, then my advice is to have people go in after a change and name the version: File > Version history > Name current version.

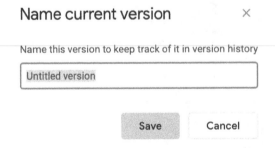

If you have someone whose old fashion—like PowerPoint, old fashion—you can also export it and email it to them. This is under File > Download as. There's all kinds of options.

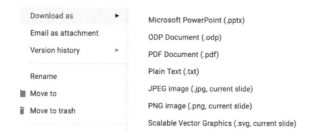

If you are giving a presentation, my advice is to export it as a PowerPoint and PDF. This way if you are ever presenting somewhere and you show up and they say, "Oh, we don't have Internet in this room—and you'll be using a computer without PowerPoint" You'll have something to display.

[4]

PRESENTING YOUR BIG IDEA!

This chapter will cover:
- Presenting to others
- Speaker notes
- Audience questions

So speaking of that big presentation, now what?! That's the easy part. See that big Present button in the right corner? Guess what that does?!

But there's more to presenting then, presenting! Click that arrow next to Present, and you'll see a few more options.

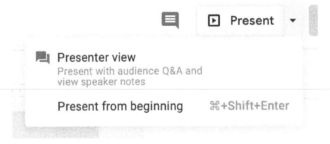

One is Presenter view, which I'll cover in just a few minutes. When your presentation is open, there's a new menu. In this menu you'll be able to turn on Q & A and notes, which will be covered below, and use the pointer. Pointer is kind of like a laser pointer; if you are doing mouse movements, then this will make it easier for viewers to watch themovements.

Using Presenter mode

By now, you've probably noticed there's a little box on the bottom that says "Click to add speaker notes." Want to take a wild guess and say what that is for? If you guessed, "Speaker notes" then congratulations, you can read!

You can actually make that area bigger or non-existent by clicking on those three dots in the middle and making it go up or down. For the sake of this book, we'll keep them right where they are.

Okay, so what are speaker notes? This is what appears on your screen when you are presenting a presentation. What do I mean by "your screen"? When you give a presentation, you usually will have your laptop connected to either a projector or TV, right? So your screen would be the laptop, and the other screen would be what it's connected to.

Speaker notes is kind of like having paper notes in front of you. It can be whatever you want. Since the audience doesn't see them, it doesn't matter—whatever is helpful when you are giving the presentation.

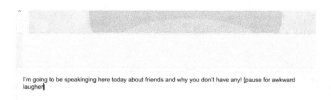

You could technically set it up to mirror your screen, but having a presenter screen is very useful. In speaker mode, you'll see the notes, the amount of time that has passed, and thumbnail of the slide coming up next, and the ability to get audience questions.

If the notes are too small for you, then you can use the "- | +" buttons to make them bigger.

ng here today about
t have any! [pause

What's really cool about presenting in Google Slides is the audience can ask questions. To accept questions while you present, you just have to turn it on. Next to speaker notes, click Audience Tools, then click the Start Now button.

There's a toggle to turn it on and off, and a link to send people.

When the person goes to that link, they are presented with a forum to ask ask their questions. They can either do it as a person or anonymously.

Other people will see it and they can upvote it or downvote it. That helps push up or down questions; a question with a 20 upvotes will be hire in the question que then a question with 2.

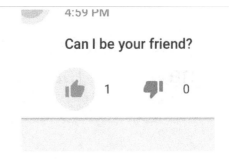

On the presenter version, they will see the question, the number of upvotes, and have an option to present it.

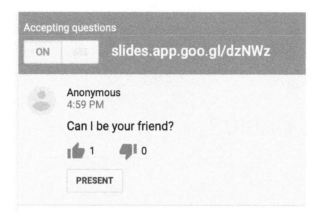

If the presenter hits the Present button, it will replace the presentation with the question.

To return to your slide, present the present button below the question again.

[5]

BEYOND THE BASICS

This chapter will cover:
- Importing and creating charts
- Creating diagrams
- Adding videos

Importing Charts from Google Sheets

Collaboration is Google Slides standout feature, as you probably can tell; something else that really makes it shine, however, is the way it interacts with other Google apps. Everything is connected through the cloud, which makes integration a breeze.

To illustrate this point, we are going to import a chart created in Google Sheets into Slides. Start off by creating a new Slide. I'll make one simple and call it The Friendly Chart.

The Friendly Chart

Now we need are chart. Open up Google Sheets, and create a basic chart. It's simple to do. Just create two columns. One with labels or names and one with data.

B	C
December 1	57
November 30	18
November 16	22
December 9	265
December 31	3.5
December 26	350
October 20	315
October 30	4
Septembe4 23	24
September 29	5
November 23	32
October 10	5
November 18	12

Next, highlight the area you are going to make a chart of, and go to Insert > Chart.

Insert Format Data Tools Add-

13 Rows **above**

13 Rows **below**

2 Columns **left**

2 Columns **right**

Cells and shift **down**

Cells and shift **right**

📊 Chart

Your chart is added right into your Sheet.

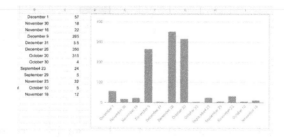

From here, click the chart and do CTRL C, which will copy it. Now go back into Google Slide, select the slide you want to add it to, and on your keyboard, hit CTRL V. This is going to ask you if you want it linked or unlinked.

Paste chart

○ Link to spreadsheet
   Only editors can update the chart. Collaborators can see a link to
   the source spreadsheet.

○ Paste unlinked

Learn more   Cancel   PASTE

Linked will connect the app to the spreadsheet, so if you update data, it will update here as well; unlinked makes it like a static image that will never change. For this example, we are doing "Link to spreadsheet."

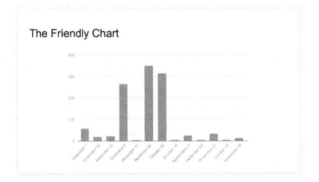

Now that it's added in, you can click on the upper right corner of the chart and have a few options. If you pick Unlink, then you will not be able to link it back, so think carefully here. Open source will let you go back in and edit the data.

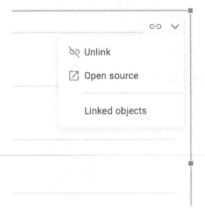

When you go back into your spreadsheet and edit the data, it will change the chart in real-time. You don't have to create a new chart.

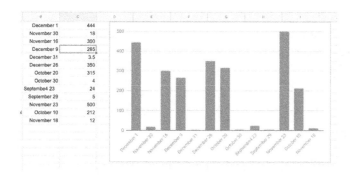

Now that it's changed in the Sheet, it will have a new option when you return to slides. Click the chart in slides. See the Update button?

Click that and it will update the chart to match what's the updated data.

Now that you've entered a caption, go ahead and open up Google Spreadsheets. We're about to do the exact same thing we did when we inserted the chart into our Google Doc. Save the chart as an image on your hard drive, and then upload it into your presentation.

If you don't have a chart and want to do it from scratch, you can also go to Insert > Chart.

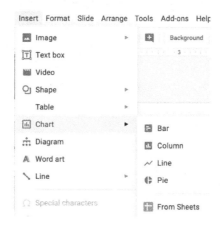

When you insert a chart from here, you will be creating a spreadsheet that's tied to the chart. It's going to add in a dummy chart; from here, you will click the menu button in the upper right corner of the dummy chart, then select "Open source."

Creating Diagrams

Diagrams aren't as common as charts, but are very resourceful when creating things like pricing tables and timelines.

To get started, create a new slide, and then go to Insert > Timeline.

What's nice about diagrams, is the hard part is already done. Google has several prebuilt templates and all you have to do is customize them a little. To start with, you'll see several different types of diagrams you can work with.

Depending on the type you select, you'll next be able to select how many dates you want to show and the color that will be used. As you update these two fields, you'll notice the preview thumbnails changing in real-time. Once you get this portion customized, select the type of diagram you want to use.

The diagram is added into your slide, and from here you can customize it to whatever suits your needs.

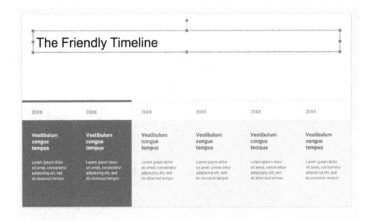

Adding Video to a Presentation

There's another app integration you can use with Google Slides. Unless you just spent the past ten years living under a rock, you've probably heard of it: YouTube.

When you add a video to Slides, you can either add a YouTube video or add one from your Google Drive. Both are easy to do, but there's a caveat here: both are online. That means if there's no Internet where you are presenting, that videos not going to load.

To get started, add another Slide, and then go to Insert > Video.

The first thing you'll see is a search bar to find your video on YouTube. That's the easiest option—especially if you don't already have a video and want to use something already created.

If you have a video on YouTube, then you can use the "By URL" option to copy in the link—this is only YouTube links, so if that video is on something like Vimeo, then you are out of luck. The last option is Google Drive. If you have a video in Google Drive, select this. Unlike photos, where if you don't have it upload it, then you can upload it directly, videos is a bit more cumbersome. You have to upload it to Google Drive, then come back and find it here. It's not complicated, but the extra step makes it a little less user friendly.

Once the video is added, right-click and select video options. This will bring up a menu with several options. The one you'll want to pay the most attention to is Format options. Under format options, you can select when the video will start and end, which is great if you only plan on showing a short clip.

You can also check off autoplay when presenting. When this is selected, the video will start as soon as you get to the slide. It can work for some videos, but if you haven't practiced the timing of your presentation, it could make for an awkward transition. If you don't check it off, then you start the video by pressing the play button.

[6]

THIS AND THAT

This chapter will cover:
- Overview of Slides menus
- Finding and using templates

The goal of this book is to get you up and running quickly; it's not to give you a comprehensive look at every feature—even the ones you will probably never used.

Before leaving you, however, I'll give you a high-level overview of some of the features not covered. Some are self-explanatory, so I'll move quick.

The view menu is what you see on the screen—do you want to see the presentation? The outline? Speaker notes? This is where you change it.

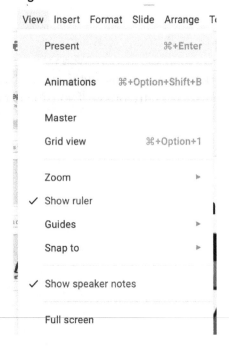

Some of the less obvious views:

Animations – we didn't cover animations in the book. Animations isn't exactly what it sounds. It's not a cartoon dancing across the screen. Think of animations like slide transitions, but for objects. So you can have the slide start, and then say "on click, I want this object to dissolve in." It's a resourceful feature, but too many animations can also make a presentation feel gimmicky, so be careful. If you want to add an animation, right-click on the image or object (object could be text) that you want to animate, and select Animate.

The animate view let's you see all of your animations, and also edit each one.

Grid view simply lays out all of your slides in a grid. It's helpful if you have dozens of slides and need to organize or print them, but not useful for shorter presentations.

Guides will turn on rulers and is useful if you need to add in something with more precision.

We've covered most of the features in the insert menu.

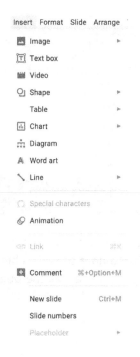

Some of the ones not covered:
- Word Art – If you've used Word, then you might be familiar with this; it makes text pop a little more by giving them a more 3D feel.

- Slide numbers – page numbers, but for slides.

Both the View and Slides menu have something called "master"; in the Slides menu it's "edit master."

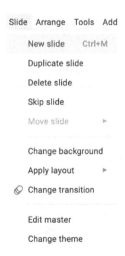

What the heck is master? It's a very technical area of slides that probably 90% of users never step foot in, but it's still good to know. This is where you can change how styles look. For example, you want to say "whenever I use a heading 1, I want it to be 30 in size, not 16." It saves you a lot of time if you are working on several presentations.

Spell checker and dictionary are found in the tools menu; that's what most people go to that menu for. If you are doing a Q & A, it's helpful to note there is a history option here. If you already gave the presentation, this is where you would go to review all the questions.

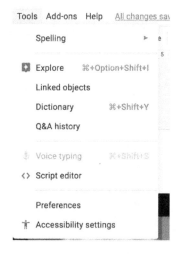

There are a lot of third party apps. This can be found in the "Add-ons menu."

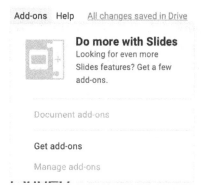

Finally, the help menu is obviously where you go for help, but there's also trainings here. These are free and very useful when you have time to learn more.

Custom Presentations from Templates

You'll recall when you first started that you could add a blank presentation or start from a template. We did blank to get started. Once you know your way around Slides, adding from a Template could save you a lot of time.

To add a template, go to your Google Drive, and select New > Google Slides > Start from a template.

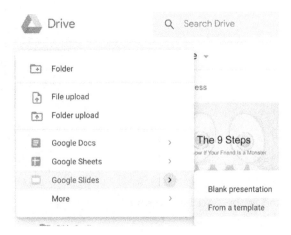

This brings up a template gallery of dozens of different presentations. The idea here is to find a style you like and then add in your own version. Don't let the names fool you. Just because it says it's a wedding template, for example, doesn't mean it's not ideal for business.

Once you select one, you'll notice right away that several slides have already been added in.

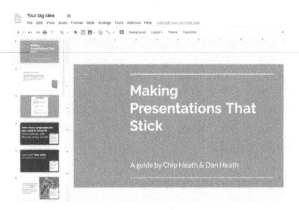

Nothing about these templates are locked in. What do I mean by that? You can change literally everything about them—images, color backgrounds, font sizes, text boxes. Now that you know your way around Slides, you'll have no problem customizing them to fit your needs.

The template gallery is nice. There's a lot there. But it's not comprehensive. I recommend browsing it, but when you are out of ideas, then go to the place with millions of ideas: Google.

Start by Googling "google slides templates."

There are only 55,000,000 results, so you'll have no problem sorting through that in no time!

In all seriousness, I do recommend browsing through some of the top matches, but I also recommend making the search specific to your industry. Such as "google slides templates for education."

People use slides for more than presentations. You can create books with it, resumes, portfolios—it's a powerful tool, so don't be afraid to think outside the box.

Once you see something you like, then download it, and then upload it to your Google Drive as a file.

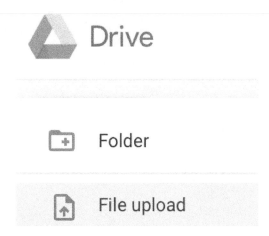

From here just right-click on the file once it's uploaded and open it as a Slide.

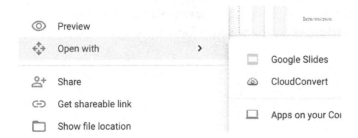

[7]

GOOGLE SLIDES KEYBOARD SHORTCUTS

You can see all the keyboard shortcuts in Google Slides by selecting Help > Keyboard shortcuts. For your reference, below are some of the most common ones you'll use.

Common actions	
New slide	Ctrl + m
Duplicate slide	Ctrl + d
Undo	Ctrl + z
Redo	Ctrl + y
	Ctrl + Shift + z
Copy	Ctrl + c
Cut	Ctrl + x
Paste	Ctrl + v
Insert or edit link	Ctrl + k
Open link	Alt + Enter
Delete	Delete
Select all	Ctrl + a
Find	Ctrl + f
Find and replace	Ctrl + h
Open...	Ctrl + o
Print	Ctrl + p
Turn on captions while presenting	Ctrl + Shift + c

Text	
Bold	Ctrl + b
Italic	Ctrl + i
Underline	Ctrl + u
Subscript	Ctrl + ,
Superscript	Ctrl + .
Strikethrough	Alt + Shift + 5
Clear formatting	Ctrl + \
	Ctrl + Space
Left align	Ctrl + Shift + l
Right align	Ctrl + Shift + r
Center align	Ctrl + Shift + e
Justify	Ctrl + Shift + j

Presenting	
Stop presenting	Esc

Next	→
Previous	←
Go to specific slide (7 followed by Enter goes to slide 7)	**Number followed by Enter**
First slide	**Home**
Last slide	**End**
Open speaker notes	s
Open audience tools	a
Toggle laser pointer	l
Print	**Ctrl + p**
Toggle captions (English only)	**Ctrl + Shift + c**
Toggle full screen	**F11**
Video Player	
Toggle play/pause	k
Rewind 10 seconds	u
Fast forward 10 seconds	o

[APPENDIX]

Lesser Used Google Apps

This chapter will cover:
- Overview of Google Drawing, Google Map, Google Sites, Google Jamboard

Other Apps

Google has four other apps bundled in their productivity suite, which won't be covered in detail here, but for your reference, I'll explain what they are. They are not covered because this guide is meant to get you started quickly and only cover commonly used features and apps—these apps are used in some industries, but not widely adopted by most people.

Google Drawing

The name "Drawing" kind of implies that this app is for all the little artists in the world—an online app to draw to your heart's content.

While you can do drawing on the app, it's not the sort of thing you use to create the next Mona Lisa. Google is collaborative software and there's not really a big market for collaborating on artwork. Instead, Google Drawing is more suited for things like flowcharts, organizational charts, wireframes, diagrams.

Google Maps

Google Maps, unlike Google Drawing, is exactly what the name implies: a Google Map.

You can use it to add pins and layers.

Google Sites

Wouldn't you love to create a website with no coding whatsoever? Well, get out from under your rock—there are lots and lots of websites for that: Squarespace, Wix, Weebly, just to name a few.

But for those who require free and ugly, there's Google Sites!

Google Sites isn't for people who want a webpage for their business. It's for people who want a very simple page that they can collaborate with others on. It would be great, for example, if you are making a fan site for your favorite TV show, and you want everyone to be a part of it.

Google Jamboard

And finally: Jamboard.

    Jamboard is basically a digital white board. If you are mounting a giant 4K TV and want to use Google, this is your solution. You can collaborate in real-time; it's perfect for business meetings and drawing cluster maps, but the hardware is too expensive for most consumers.

PART 3: GOOGLE FOR THE CLASSROOM

INTRODUCTION

Every tech company wants to be in the business of education. It's a powerful space—there's always a need for people learning.

While companies like Microsoft and Apple have competed in this space with hardware and software, Google took it a step further by creating a cloud-based classroom for teachers.

There's hardware (Chromebooks) and software (Google Apps) too, but Google Classroom is a unique environment where teachers can connect in a private space with other teachers, students, and parents.

[1]

GETTING STARTED

This chapter will cover:
- What is Google for Classroom?
- Creating your first class
- Inviting students / teachers to join

Similar to other online teaching platforms like Blackboard, Google Classroom allows teachers to post announcements, share documents, and create and grade tests. The selling point for Google Classroom over other platforms is its cost—or lack thereof; Google Classroom is free…sort of! Anyone with a Google account can use the platform, but only schools with a free G Suite for Education can take full advantage of it. Some administrative features will not be enabled.

Using Classroom at a school with students?

If so, your school must sign up for a free G Suite for Education account before you can use Classroom. Learn More

G Suite for Education lets schools decide which Google services their students can use, and provides additional privacy and security protections that are important in a school setting. Students cannot use Google Classroom at a school with personal accounts.

☐ I've read and understand the above notice, and I'm not using Classroom at a school with students

GO BACK   CONTINUE

This does not mean you cannot use it if you are using it as a non-school. If you are a homeschooling parent, you can still make Google Classroom work for you.

Why is it free? There are a number of reasons, but the biggest one is it promotes Google's free Google Apps services (which includes Google Docs, Google Sheets, and Google Slides).

Getting Started

To get started, head over to classroom.google.com. If you are a teacher that is using this for school, make sure you are logged in to your Google for Education account—not your personal account:

Next, click the + button in the upper right corner, and Create class.

Create or join your first class!

The easiest way to know if your school has Google for Education is when you add the class, you won't see the box asking if you are a school. It will go straight to the pop-up asking you for your class's information. The only thing required here is the class name (which can be anything). The other three fields are optional:

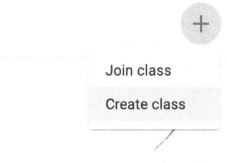

If you add a subject, you'll see it start predicting what you want as you type. You also can type something not already here.

Computer

AP Computer Science A

AP Computer Science Principles

Introduction to Computer Programming

Computer Repair

Computer Science Club

Your first class will now be in what Google calls the "stream." I'll show you how to access multiple classes later in the book.

There are a number of things you can edit here. The first place you'll probably want to start is the look of the class page—after all, the bowling balls don't exactly represent what the class is about. To update the look, click on Select theme. Google breaks down multiple subjects with multiple images/themes in each one:

If you don't like any of these Themes, select the option under it: Upload photo. This lets you upload a photo from your computer:

Because the theme area is not a full-size image, you'll probably be able to select only an area of the photo. Notice the image below—only a portion is available, so I have to position the box over the area that I want:

After I do that and save the image, my theme has now changed—if you have students in your class, this image will change for them as well.

If you have multiple classes, then you can click the arrows facing different directions to toggle between them:

I created a fake class to illustrate what it will look like when you click this button:

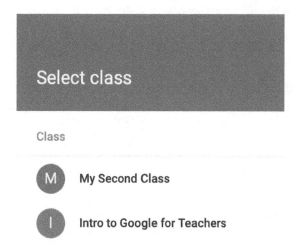

Click the down arrow on the header image and it will show additional information about the class:

There are two ways to enroll students into your class. Invite them or give them a unique code. The unique code is covered in the image below, but it is next to where it says Class code. Click the broken box next to that and it will expand. Click the box in the lower right corner of that box, and it will enlarge even further:

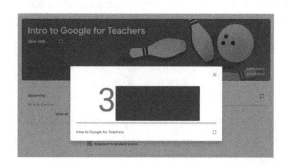

A student will take this code and go to classroom.google.com and then click the + button in the upper right corner and select Join class and type in the Class code:

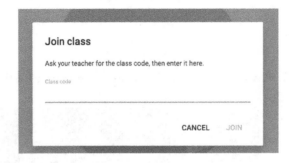

To invite a person to the class, go to People on the top menu bar. You'll be able to add two types of people: Teachers and students. Click the person with the plus button next to the type of person that you want to add:

Teachers   &+

Students   &+

Once you add the person and they accept the invitation (they'll get an email and will have to accept it before they are officially added—it will only say invited if they haven't accepted). Once they're added, you can go here to email a student by clicking on the three dots next to their name:

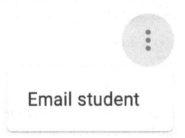

You can also email the entire class by selecting the checkbox above all your students (which selects all), clicking the Actions button, and selecting Email. You can also use the Action to remove every student from the class. Or just check the students you want to remove and go to Actions and remove or email (if you want to perform the action only on selected students).

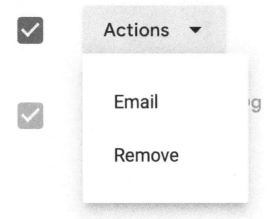

[2]

CLASSWORK

This chapter will cover:
- Where to add assignments / classwork
- Starting discussions
- Posting lectures
- Grading assignments

Now that you have students in the class, you are ready to start assigning classwork. Click the Classwork button in the top menu to get started. Because we haven't created anything yet, this area is going to look different once you go back in and there are assignments.

Before I dig into creating classwork, I'll point out two things. The first is Google Calendar. Click on that:

Every class you create has its own calendar. So, when you click on it, you'll see over on the left side that there's a new calendar checked off:

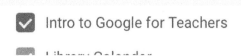

Click the three dots to the right of that and you can hide it or change the settings:

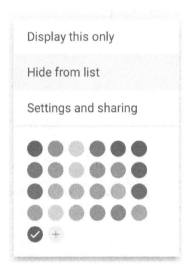

Clicking on the settings brings up a whole other slew of settings. You can, for example, only share it with certain people:

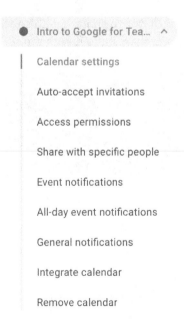

You can also go in and add descriptions for the class, change the time zone, and much more:

The second thing I'll point out: Class Drive folder. Click on that:

This opens up your Google Drive. Every class gets its own folder. This is where you'll store lectures, videos, class photos, or anything else you need the class to see:

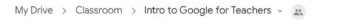

If you click the people button, you'll get to share it with specific people. For example, you could create a new folder just for parents and then share it with them:

Back to creating the actual course work. Click the Create button:

When you click it, you'll see all the types of course work you can create—some will be graded and some will not:

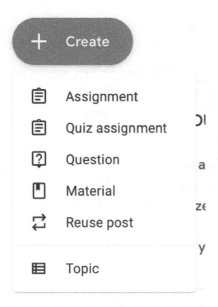

We will start with Assignments. Here you can name your assignment and put in a description:

Next to For is a drop-down box that says All students. When you click that, there's an option to select what student(s) it goes to. By default, it goes to all students, but if you are creating an alternative assignment for one student, then you could just create it for one specific student:

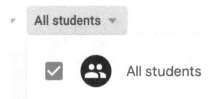

On the bottom of this pop-up is an area to add points. How many is entirely up to you. By default, everything is 100 points:

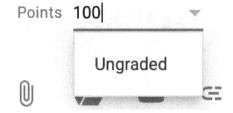

You might be able to describe the assignment using the box above, but many assignments will require other things—photos, videos, links, etc. That's where the next set of buttons below the points will come in handy. The paperclip is an attachment from your computer, the one next to that is an attachment from Google Drive, the Play button is to insert a YouTube video, and the last is to add a link to something:

When you click the Assign button, it asks you if you want to assign it right away or just schedule it. This lets you plan out your entire class in advance, but have students see the assignments as they are scheduled:

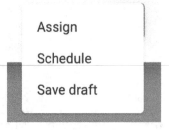

Once it's assigned, your News section will look different. Students will also see this assignment right away in their portal:

News   ⋮

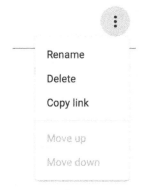

Click the three dots and you'll be able to rename it or delete it:

Quizzes

The next option is for Quizzes. If you have ever used Google Forms, this should be a breeze for you. Quizzes are Google Forms:

To get to the form (or quiz), click on the Blank Quiz at the bottom of the box:

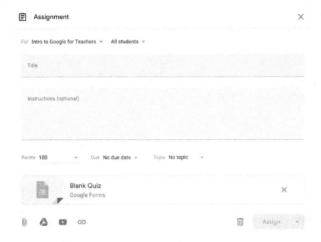

If you've never used Google Forms, then you can go to the section of this guide on Google Forms for an overview of how it works.

Questions

The next option is Question. Question is meant to be something other students can see, so think of it like a forum. It's a good place to make the course more interactive. You have the choice of making the question something other students can reply to. To make sure students are actively contributing, you might instruct them to answer the question, and then comment on three other students' answers. Like other assignments, you can make this for all students, or select students, and give it a due date:

Material

Material is not meant to be turned in. The best way to describe it is lesson resources. Students read or view it, and you might reference it in assignments, but students don't actually turn anything in:

Topics

Once you have added assignments, it's a good idea to add topics:

Topics let you group your assignments. So, you could have, for example, five topics and each one could have several different assignments, lectures, and questions. Once the topic is created, then you can drag assignments into it (see below). Additionally, you can create the topics, and then classwork— as you create the classwork, there is an option to add in the topic.

Organizing Questions and Assignments

Now that there are multiple classwork questions/assignments you can click those three dots to the right of the classwork to move it up or down. If you need to edit anything, you can click on the classwork's name.

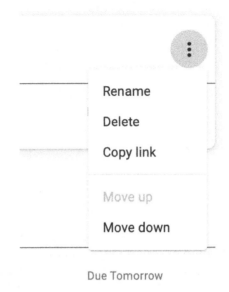

Due Tomorrow

On the left side, you'll see that topics have been added to the navigation menu:

All topics

Sample Topics

News

Turning in Classwork

When a student logs into their portal, they'll see all the classwork they need to turn in:

This student has opened up the Questions assignment and answered Green:

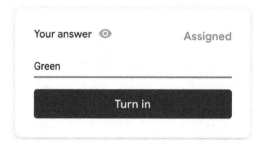

When they (or other students) go to completed answers, they'll see the answer:

For actual assignments that require something to be turned in besides questions, they will have the option to either share a link or Google Drive location, or upload it as a file from their computer:

Back on the teacher end of the portal, you'll be able to see all the answers, and also have the ability to grade it:

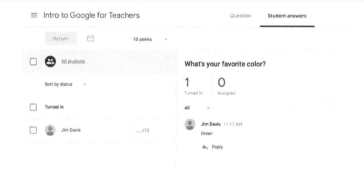

You can also mute a student by clicking on the three dots:

Grading Classwork

You can start grading student work by clicking on Grades from the top menu. Here you'll see a list of all your students with rows for each assignment:

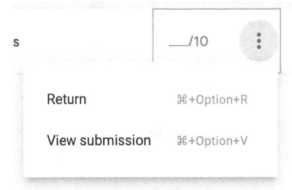

When you click the three dots next to the number, you can view the submission:

Go ahead and assign grades to each assignment. Notice how it has Draft in italics? That means you have added a grade but haven't submitted it:

To submit it, click the three dots and click Return. Here, you can also add any private comments for the student:

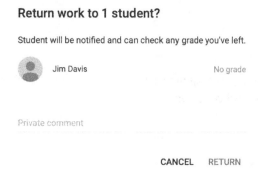

Once you add the grade, it will no longer be in green. If you decide to change the grade, just click on the grade (10 in this case) and add in the new score; once you do that, you need to return it to the student once more:

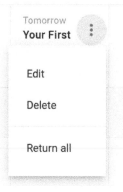

If you click the three dots on the top of the row, you can also return it to all students at once:

Click the three dots a second time and you can view submissions, which lets you see all grades. In view submissions, you can also download all grades into a CSV or Google Sheet.

When you click the three lines on the left corner, you'll be able to see all the classes you are teaching. You can also see a To-do list:

The To-do area helps keep you organized; you can see all the assignments from all your classes and review what's been turned in and graded:

[3]

BEYOND BASICS

This chapter will cover:
- To-do lists
- Ending classes
- Archiving classes
- Copying / repeating classes

To-Do List

Once you've reviewed everything, just click the three dots to the right of it and mark them as reviewed:

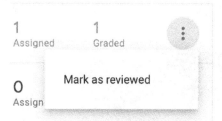

Also in that side menu, you can access your overall class settings (for all classes—not just one). This lets you toggle on/off different settings—such as if you are notified that a student is late with work:

Finally, on the side, there's a calendar. This lets you see what you have going on in your classes throughout the week:

This applies to all classes. If you only want to change the setting of one class, then go to the side menu, select the class you want to edit or go into the settings of, and click the config button:

On this page, you'll be able to change the name of the class, or any other details:

If you scroll all the way to the bottom, you can change the way the grading system for your class works and add categories:

Ending, Archiving, and Copying a Class

The class is over. Now what? Rejoice! And then finalize everything in Google Classroom, so you can repeat the class and have less work the next semester or school year.

Open up that side menu again, and this time click on classes:

This gives you a high-level overview of all of your classes. Down at the bottom of the overview is a chart arrow, which launches into your grading; next to that is a folder, which opens into your class Google Drive:

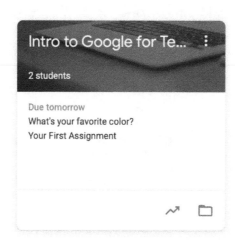

If you click the three dots in the upper right corner, you'll have several options. One is archive. Click that:

It will give you a message confirming your choice (remember, you can undo this later); basically it's letting you know that students can no longer make any changes or turn anything in. If you are ready, then hit archive again:

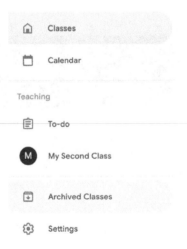

If you go back to that side menu again, you'll see there's now an option called Archived Classes. Click that:

It looks the same as your active class, but there are now lines going through it:

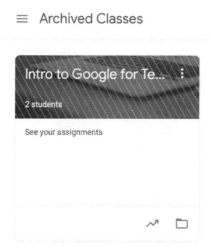

Click the three dots, and there's a new option: Restore and Delete. Restore puts it back in your active classes, so it's essentially an undo; Delete permanently erases it:

When you choose Delete, it will confirm your choice and tell you all your posts and comments will be gone, but files will still be in the Google Drive. Unlike archiving a class, this cannot be undone:

If you know you are teaching the class again, then before you delete it (you can also do this before you archive it), click the three dots, and select copy:

This creates a duplicate of the class so all your topics and assignments will be copied over. The only thing not copied over are the students and any announcements:

Copy class

Create a new class with copied topics and classwork items. Rosters and announcements won't be copied.

Class name (required)

Copy of Intro to Google for Teachers

Section

Subject

AP Computer Science A

Room

CANCEL   COPY

[4]

GOOGLE FORMS

This chapter will cover:
* Using Google Forms

Like most things in Google Apps, Google Forms is pretty straightforward. The below how-to shows you just how it works.

I'm going to walk you through how you would create a form from scratch. This is done outside of Google for Classroom. Go to drive.google.com.

If you click that "More" option when you are creating a new document, one very handy application you'll see is "Google Forms."

Google Forms lets you create custom surveys. It's very simple and resourceful. Once you click on a blank form to get started, you see a screen like this:

The first question is already there. You just have to name everything—the name of the form, and what the question is. By default, it's multiple choice, but if you click the multiple-choice dropdown, you'll get several other options:

To add a new question, just click the "+" on the side menu:

It will add the question under the previous, but you can change its position by clicking the six small boxes to drag it above (or if there's multiple questions, below).

You can also use that side menu, to add links, text, images, YouTube videos, and sections. When you are done with your form and you want to share it, click the send button:

This will bring up a box that lets you specify how you will share it: by email, link, or embedded on a webpage:

To toggle between each, just click the icon that represents how you want to see it. The middle, for example (seen below), is by link; the < > is to embed in a webpage.

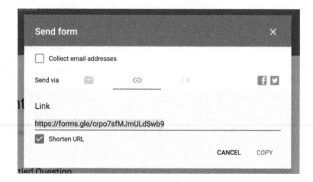

When you embed into a webpage, you'll be able to customize the size:

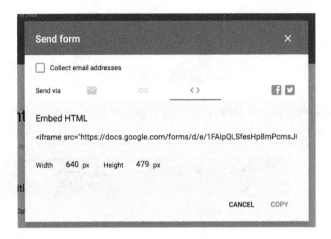

ABOUT THE AUTHOR

Scott La Counte is a librarian and writer. His first book, *Queit, Please: Dispatches from a Public Librarian* (Da Capo 2008) was the editor's choice for the Chicago Tribune and a Discovery title for the Los Angeles Times; in 2011, he published the YA book The N00b Warriors, which became a #1 Amazon bestseller; his most recent book is *#OrganicJesus: Finding Your Way to an Unprocessed, GMO-Free Christianity* (Kregel 2016).

He has written dozens of best-selling how-to guides on tech products.

You can connect with him at ScottDouglas.org.

CPSIA information can be obtained
at www.ICGtesting.com
Printed in the USA
BVHW091143200820
586901BV00017B/2972